Encouragement
for Today

Encouragement
for Today

devotions for everyday living

Renee Swope, Lysa TerKeurst, Samantha Evilsizer

and the Proverbs 31 Team

ZONDERVAN

Encouragement for Today
Copyright © 2013 by Proverbs 31 Ministries

This title is also available as a Zondervan ebook. Visit www.zondervan.com/ebooks.

This title is also available in a Zondervan audio edition. Visit www.zondervan.fm.

Requests for information should be addressed to:
Zondervan, *Grand Rapids, Michigan 49530*

Library of Congress Cataloging-in-Publication Data

Swope, Renee, 1967–
    Encouragement for today : devotions for everyday living / Renee Swope, Lysa
TerKeurst, Samantha Evilsizer, and the Proverbs 31 Ministries Team.
        pages cm
        ISBN 978-0-310-33628-0 (softcover)
        1. Christian women—Prayers and devotions. 2. Christian women—Religious life.
    I. Title.
    BV4844.S96   2013
    242'.643—dc23   2013013058

Published in association with the literary agency of Fedd & Company, Inc., Post Office Box 341973, Austin, TX 78734.

Cover design: Studio Gearbox
Cover photography: Veer®
Interior design: Beth Shagene

Printed in the United States of America

---

13 14 15 16 17 18 19 /DCI/ 23 22 21 20 19 18 17 16 15 14 13 12 11 10 9 8 7 6 5 4 3

*To the women who begin each day with us
in God's Word through our daily email devotions
and to the women on our team who write them.*

Contents

Acknowledgments

Jesus, thank You for allowing us to serve You by sharing with women Your Word each morning through our devotions. We pray this book will be an offering that brings You honor and glory. Thank You for the gift of Your Word that transforms us, Your Spirit that encourages us, and Your wisdom that leads us.

To our amazing husbands JJ, Art, and Joshua, thank you for the sacrifices you make while we serve Jesus through Proverbs 31 Ministries. But more than anything, thank you for the way you love and lead us, and the way you live out the gospel each and every day.

Thank you to our Proverbs 31 Ministries staff: Melissa, Teri, Wendy P., Sheila, Barb, Lisa C., Angie, Lisa B., Lindsay, Lori, Leah, Natalie, Kenisha, Van, Meredith, Glynnis, Karen, Laurie, Janet, Kim, and Alison. Also, to our volunteers who serve behind the scenes so faithfully. We love that together we all get to touch the lives of millions of women across the world each day. We couldn't do it without you!

It is with hearts full of gratitude that we thank the team at Zondervan for all you've done. We have so enjoyed working with you: Sandy Vander Zicht, Greg Clouse, Alicia Mey, Curt Diepenhorst, Joyce Ondersma, Merideth Bliss, Jennifer VerHage, Tracy Danz, and Sarah Johnson.

Thank you, Esther Fedorkevich, for believing in this project and working behind the scenes to help our dream become a reality!

To our friends at Crosswalk, BibleGateway, Family Christian Bookstores, and Growthtrac who partner with us each weekday to bring the hope of Christ and the life-changing power of His Word to women's everyday lives through our *Encouragement for Today* devotions. We are forever grateful for you!

Don't Despise the Small Stuff

Lysa TerKeurst

Who is wise and understanding among you?
Let them show it by their good life,
by deeds done in the humility that comes from wisdom.
(JAMES 3:13)

What seems small in your world? By small, I mean that place where your vision is grand but your reality isn't. Is it your influence? Your opportunity? Your business? Your ability to give? Your ministry?

Look at that small place. What do you see?

If what you see is less than encouraging, might you take the bold step of looking at it again? Because hidden within that smallness is a gift—one that will yield wisdom you can't get any other way. If you look closely enough at what seems small in your world, you'll begin to see how "deeds done in the humility that comes from wisdom" will create something new in you.

This small place in your world is where humility is birthed. Humility is that glorious and rare quality that doesn't take too much credit. Humility knows real success is laced with heavenward glances, bent knees, and whispered praises to the One. The only One.

He who gives.

And He who withholds. Not out of spite, not out of ignorance, not out of deafness, and certainly not out of comparisons in which others are found to be more deserving. No. He withholds out of protection. With loving restraint, He withholds the big to protect the hidden workings of the small. The small we should not despise. It is in these humble places where we experience the quiet nurture, the holy unfolding, the deep stirrings that draw us closer to the heart of God.

Soon, the soul must choose: haughtiness or humility.

If that soul has never tasted small, it will never develop a humble palate. It will crave only big, until it is so full of big that being big inflates and distorts and never satisfies.

But for the soul that has dined on what is small, humility becomes the richest fare. The taste that satisfies. The thing most desired to be consumed. All things humble will eventually be made great.

Oh, the beautiful gift of small!

There is great delight in knowing the truth about what small really is. Small isn't a belittling of one's calling or a diminishment of one's future. It's simply a place—a grand but unnoticed place. A place we need to protect and remember because it keeps all things big in proper perspective.

Small isn't what keeps us *from* our grand vision. Small is what keeps us *for* our grand vision.

Dear Lord, help me to embrace the small. I want to see with Your eyes what You have planned for me. In Jesus' name, Amen.

REMEMBER

This small place in your world is where humility is birthed. Small isn't what keeps us *from* our grand vision. Small is what keeps us *for* our grand vision.

REFLECT

When in the past have you "dined on what is small"? How did it feel in the moment? How do you feel about that experience now? What have you learned? How have you grown?

RESPOND

Choose one thing today that you will do "small." Fold and put away your husband's laundry. Bring your boss coffee. Pull your neighbor's trash to the curb. Whatever you choose, ask the Lord to increase your taste for the "small" while you're performing it.

POWER VERSES

Proverbs 22:4; Psalm 37:11

Lord, I Want to Know You

Renee Swope

Those who know your name trust you, O LORD,
because you have never deserted those who seek your help.
(PSALM 9:10 GW)

I had heard great things about LeAnn, but I didn't really know her until we worked together. And the more I was with her, the more I discovered traits I admired and enjoyed—especially her dry sense of humor and unique way of making people feel noticed and loved. As our friendship deepened, I also learned LeAnn was dependable—something I discovered only when I needed her help and she came through for me.

I've found my relationship with God grows in a similar way. Whatever I may know about God, I won't really know God personally until I spend time with Him and depend on Him. I learn to trust His heart by interacting with Him and experiencing His character in personal ways.

The book of Judges features a fascinating story that illustrates how this same dynamic happened in the life of a man named Gideon. No one expected much of Gideon, including Gideon himself. He belonged to a weak tribe and described himself as the least important member in his family (Judges 6:15). So it was not surprising that he was somewhat skeptical when the angel of the Lord appeared to him, called him a mighty warrior, and announced he would defeat a powerful enemy army. At this point, Gideon only knew *about* God. He had heard of God's faithfulness in other people's lives, but he didn't know God personally.

Asking for a sign that it really was the Lord talking, Gideon obediently set out a meal of bread and meat. When the angel touched them with the tip of his staff, fire flared from the rock on which the meal sat, consuming the food. Instantly, Gideon realized this individual was indeed the angel of the Lord. "Alas, Sovereign LORD!" he exclaimed, "I have seen the angel of the LORD face to face!" (Judges 6:22).

Gideon was terrified. Immediately, the Lord said to him, "Peace! Do not be afraid. You are not going to die" (Judges 6:23). Then "Gideon built an altar to the LORD there and called it The LORD Is Peace" (Judges 6:24).

God revealed His character by demonstrating His power and by giving Gideon peace. Now Gideon not only knew about God, he knew God personally.

Just like my relationship with LeAnn has deepened as I've gotten to know her better, my relationship with Jesus has grown over time. I've come to love Him more as I've experienced His unfailing love for me. I've learned to trust Him as I've gotten to know His heart and His character. And it's much easier to trust someone I know.

One way to know God better is to focus on one of the Bible's names for God. For example, if we want to know God as our healer, we pray to *Jehovah Rapha* and ask for the healing we need—spiritually, emotionally, mentally, or physically. If we want to know God as our provider, we pray to *Jehovah Jireh*, ask Him to meet our needs each day, and then look for His provisions.

We will grow in our relationship with Jesus and our confidence in Him will deepen as we live in this promise: "Those who know your name trust you, O LORD, because you have never deserted those who seek your help" (Psalm 9:10 GW).

Dear Lord, I want to know You by name and experience the fullness of all that You are. Help me trust and follow You more and more each day. In Jesus' name, Amen.

REMEMBER

We learn to trust God's heart by interacting with Him and experiencing His character in personal ways.

REFLECT

What captivates you about God's names?

RESPOND

Keep a list of God's names with you to remind you of who He is.*

POWER VERSES

Proverbs 18:10; Genesis 22:13–14; Judges 6:24

---

*See Appendix A for a helpful list of the names of God.

Found Hope

Nicki Koziarz

For whatever was written in earlier times was written for our instruction,
so that through perseverance and the encouragement
of the Scriptures we might have hope.

(ROMANS 15:4 NASB)

We were out of options the day the sheriff's car pulled into our driveway. After a series of unfortunate events, things had gone from bad to worse to hopeless.

The officer's smile did nothing to relieve the discomfort of this dreadful moment. As she handed me the papers, I began to cry. Acknowledging the baby in my arms and the toddler peeking out from behind me, she kindly said, "I'm sorry."

"Thank you," I whispered, as I slowly closed the door.

I read through the official documents. Elaborate legal terms, laws I didn't understand, and words in bold letters conveyed the dreadful news: "You must vacate the premises within thirty days."

Foreclosure.

It was unwanted and unavoidable. It felt shameful and embarrassing. It launched our family into an aching process of letting go.

The carefully painted mustard-yellow walls: I would miss them. How would I survive without the afternoon play dates with my neighbor and her children? And what about all those economical hot dog dinners my husband and I ate so we could save just a little more to buy this home?

Any hope I had left faded fast. Hope wasn't something I could muster on my own. I knew I needed access to a greater hope — the kind of hope the apostle Paul describes: "For whatever was written in earlier times was written for our instruction, so that through perseverance and the encouragement of the Scriptures we might have hope" (Romans 15:4 NASB).

During this devastating season of broken dreams, I needed the deep, historical roots of hope the Bible offers. I could find hope because Abraham and Sarah found hope by believing God would give them a child in their old age (Genesis 15, 17–18). I could find hope because Ruth and

Naomi found hope by trusting God would provide for them after they lost their husbands (Ruth 3). I could find hope because Mary and Martha found hope when Jesus raised their brother from the dead (John 11).

As I closed the door to our home for the last time, I accepted this place of brokenness. But I also made a choice to find hope no matter what. I found hope when my daughters excitedly explored our new rental home. I found hope when my mom cheerfully helped unpack our boxes. I found hope when my husband's heart drew closer to mine through this difficult experience.

Hope is at the core of our faith in Christ. As we allow His hope to flow into us, it will flow through us even in the most difficult circumstances. If you are struggling today, take heart. Look back at those in the pages of Scripture who had hope. Allow their hope to give you courage and hope for your future. Hope heals our broken dreams.

Dear Lord, thank You for the hope You give me to heal the broken places in my life. I ask that You would give me the strength to find hope today. In Jesus' name, Amen.

REMEMBER

When life's broken places lead us to Jesus, ultimately we will find hope.

REFLECT

Why do you think it is so challenging to find hope in the midst of our dark circumstances?

RESPOND

If you are feeling hopeless, reach out to a friend or two. Ask your friends to share an experience in which God gave them hope.

POWER VERSES

1 Peter 1:3; Romans 5:5

Into Her Pain

Samantha Evilsizer

"A Samaritan traveling the road came on him.
When he saw the man's condition, his heart went out to him."

(LUKE 10:33 MSG)

My friend was suffering. She didn't have to say a word; I could see it all in her eyes: *I need someone to crawl into my pit with me. I need someone to help me out of the pain.*

I felt a lump in my throat as she poured out her grief. Circumstances had beaten her down and left her emotionally half dead on the side of life's road. Obvious quick-fix phrases darted across my mind: *Time heals all wounds. What doesn't kill you makes you stronger. God's timing is perfect.* I recognized them for what they were — a way to ease my own discomfort and bypass her pain.

"But when he saw the man lying there, he crossed to the other side of the road and passed him by" (Luke 10:31 NLT).

I didn't want to disrespect my friend with a walk-by — stepping over her pain with thoughtless words. Words withheld are better than careless words. Clichés offer no comfort. *Be still. Listen. Administer mercy.*

"A Samaritan traveling the road came on him. When he saw the man's condition, his heart went out to him" (Luke 10:33 MSG).

Comfort comes from a still presence, a listening ear, a merciful hand. Comfort couples the truth of God's Word with merciful deeds. Comfort answers the call to step into the pit.

"He gave him first aid, disinfecting and bandaging his wounds. Then he lifted him onto his donkey, led him to an inn, and made him comfortable" (Luke 10:34 MSG). The Good Samaritan loved with what resources he had.

My friend's healing journey began that night as we sat together and she poured out her pain. I didn't have much to give her, but a simple offering from a willing heart is capable of great things. I listened and administered mercy. "You will learn to trust again, to believe in goodness again." Later, others offered counsel, covered her in prayer, and spoke words of truth. Together, we tucked arms under our friend, lifted her up and out of the pit.

"In the morning he took out two silver coins and gave them to the innkeeper, saying, 'Take good care of him. If it costs any more, put it on my bill—I'll pay you on my way back'" (Luke 10:35 MSG).

Years later, I was the one who landed in the pit. My heart cracked open and I fell headlong into pain. My friend crossed the road to me. She offered a still presence, a listening ear, a merciful hand. "You'll heal," she said. "Once more, you'll believe God has good plans for you."

Then she winked at me and smiled. "Someone once told me that, and she was right," she said. "I believe again. I trust again." She wrapped her arms of mercy around me. I knew it was time to leave the pit, time to heal.

"'Now which of these three would you say was a neighbor to the man who was attacked by bandits?' Jesus asked. The man replied, 'The one who showed him mercy.' Then Jesus said, 'Yes, now go and do the same'" (Luke 10:36–37 NLT).

Dear Lord, thank You for Your healing mercy. Teach me to be still, to listen, and to administer mercy. In Jesus' name, Amen.

REMEMBER

A simple offering from a willing heart is capable of restoring hope. Be still; listen; administer mercy.

REFLECT

In what pits have you stayed, not allowing in truth, help, or healing?

RESPOND

Is there someone you know who is hurting? Cross the road to them and be still, listen, and administer mercy in a specific way. This may mean taking a meal, calling them, or sharing a Bible verse.

POWER VERSES

Micah 6:8; Galatians 6:2

Being Thankful Changes Everything

Lysa TerKeurst

*For our struggle is not against flesh and blood, but against the rulers,
against the authorities, against the powers of this dark world
and against the spiritual forces of evil in the heavenly realms.*

(EPHESIANS 6:12)

I sat on the bed, tears streaming down my face, negative thoughts racing through my mind. Why does marriage have to be so hard sometimes? Why won't he change? Maybe I married the wrong man. I was discouraged, overwhelmed, and tempted to give up.

This scene was repeated again and again the first five years of our marriage. But here I am nineteen years later, thankful I didn't walk away.

Over the years I've learned that my husband isn't my enemy. Art may feel like my enemy, but Satan is the real enemy who hates marriage and schemes against my husband and me. Satan's goal is to cast something between two people in order to cause a separation. Satan wants to separate us with conflict, hurt feelings, misunderstandings, and frustration of all kinds. He wants to separate us from our neighbors, our friends, our coworkers, our parents, our spouses, our kids. He wants to separate us from God's heart.

One of the strategic ways Satan initiates a separation is by luring us into a place of complaining. If he can get us to focus on what is aggravating and negative in life, little cracks of distance start forming in our relationships. The grass starts looking greener everywhere except where we are standing.

I can see this clearly when I look back on the first five years of my marriage. Somehow, I became hyperfocused on all I felt was wrong with my husband and blinded to all that was good. I complained and nagged and set out to change him. And I almost destroyed my marriage in the process.

Satan had a field day as the distance between Art and me kept widening. We went to counseling, but my heart was so hurt—and hardened—that I refused to connect on any level. I was bitter and miserable.

One day as I was in a fit of tears asking God to please make things better, I felt challenged to start listing things about Art for which I was thankful. It was hard at first. But with each positive quality I listed, my perspective slowly changed. It was as if the clouds of negativity lifted and I could see his good qualities once again.

How sad that I had spent five years thinking my marriage was the pits. Now I know marriage with my Art is better when I'm investing in it and seeing the whole picture. And being thankful—intentionally listing things for which I am grateful—is a great way to start.

Dear Lord, thank You for helping me to be aware and appreciative of the good qualities in those I love. Help me to recognize Satan's schemes and combat them with the power of a thankful heart. In Jesus' name, Amen.

REMEMBER

Satan wants to separate us with conflict, hurt feelings, misunderstandings, and frustration of all kinds. We can combat him by recognizing his schemes and changing our perspective.

REFLECT

When did you last thank God for someone important in your life, such as your husband, children, family, or friends? Do negative thoughts toward them seep into your words and actions? Be honest with yourself and determine why you're so negative toward them.

RESPOND

Take a moment right now to sort out your thoughts toward one specific person. For each negative, "separating" thought about him or her, intentionally combat it with something for which you are thankful about that person.

POWER VERSES

Philippians 4:6; 2 Corinthians 4:15

A One-Cup Life

Glynnis Whitwer

There is a time for everything,
and a season for every activity under the heavens.
(ECCLESIASTES 3:1)

Flour-dusted shirts, sticky hands, and two happy little faces gathered in my kitchen for an afternoon of baking. The counters were covered with bowls, spoons, and ingredients as my young daughters scooped, measured, and stirred their way through a Baking 101 lesson.

Part of the learning process involved reading the recipe. So when the recipe called for 1½ cups of milk, I asked my youngest daughter to retrieve the two-cup liquid measure. She made it to the right cabinet, but mistakenly picked out the one-cup measure.

Instead of sending her back to the cabinet, I demonstrated how to make the one-cup measure work. But I also wanted my daughters to understand why we had to make the adjustment. I needed them to know that they couldn't put 1½ cups of liquid into a one-cup container.

Later, it occurred to me that this principle of measurement applied to more than just milk. How many of us routinely try to cram twelve hours' worth of tasks into an eight-hour workday? We say yes to more activities than we have time for, and take on more responsibilities than we have energy for. Then we wonder why we can't find a healthy balance to life.

For years I tried to put too much into my schedule. "Yes" slipped off my tongue with little thought and no prayer. I'd collapse at night, exhausted and annoyed. It was a hard way to live, as I constantly felt like there was one more thing I should be doing. And even what I did accomplish never seemed enough.

My breakthrough came one day when I decided to write down everything I had to do on one piece of paper—which soon became two. I included everything: phone calls I needed to make, emails I needed to send, projects I needed to start, and more projects I needed to finish. The list included tasks for that day as well as things I had to do for projects due in upcoming months.

Reviewing the list left me feeling overwhelmed, but it also brought some relief. Once my responsibilities were in one place, the problem was obvious. I was trying to fit 1½ cups' worth of commitments into a one-cup life.

I knew I had to simplify and let some things go. It wasn't easy, but after a year of cutting back on commitments, I finally had a more manageable, focused, and productive life. With every subtraction, I gained an additional measure of peace.

In the process, I learned I always have exactly enough time to do what God wants me to do: "There is a time for everything, and a season for every activity under the heavens" (Ecclesiastes 3:1). The key to balance is seeking God's will for me in this season, and not spending time on assignments meant for other people.

Overcommitting myself is always a temptation. But with God's wisdom and an updated list of all my commitments, I get ongoing reality checks that help me make wise decisions. And although I'm not really good at math, I know that a cup and a half of something will never fit in a one-cup container.

Dear Lord, You have uniquely created me and equipped me for the service You've determined. And yet so many times I try to take on responsibility that's not mine. Help me to be content with my assignment and to work at it joyfully. In Jesus' name, Amen.

REMEMBER

To live a balanced life, we need to make sure our commitments match our available time and energy.

REFLECT

What factors typically lead you to overcommit yourself?

RESPOND

Consider those responsibilities over which you have control. Which ones should be pruned from your schedule?

POWER VERSES

Isaiah 26:3; 1 Peter 5:8

Silencing My Soul

Wendy Pope

But I have stilled and quieted my soul.

(PSALM 131:2 NIV 1984)

I'm a talker; always have been. When report cards were sent home, my parents never expected anything better than a C beside the word "conduct." One of my elementary teachers politely called me "very social," but most were more blunt. "Wendy talks too much. She could learn more if she talked less."

Unfortunately, old habits die hard. I brought this trait of talking too much into my quiet time with God, filling the silence with words — lots and lots of words. Sometimes I wonder if the Father looks at the Son and says, "I can't get a word in edgewise with this girl! She could learn more if she talked less."

I wanted to tell God about all the good solutions He could implement to solve my problems. To-do lists, not peace and quiet, ran through my head. I was perpetually distracted by shelves that needed dusting and piles of toys that needed to be put away. It felt unnatural not to be talking to God, so I resisted being still and quiet.

I shared my uneasiness about silence with God, but I knew that silence and stillness were things He was inviting me to. During these times, I sensed God's gentle encouragement. *Shhh. Be still. It's okay to be silent. You don't have to say a word.*

Gradually, I settled into a habit of just being with God. It was something I felt but couldn't initially describe until I read the psalmist's words: "I have stilled and quieted my soul" (Psalm 131:2 NIV 1984). *Rest.* That was the name for what I experienced in the silence. God united His heart with mine, allowing me to experience the rest I needed.

As we fill the reservoir of our souls with true refreshment from God, we learn to relax in the rhythms of His grace. We experience real peace and rest that only come from the silence and stillness of being with Him. We carry this refreshment with us as we face the challenges of our days.

Do you have the gift of gab like me? Do you find it challenging to sit quietly with God? Ask Him to help you not only to practice but also to enjoy silence and stillness. Your soul will find refreshing peace. God's rest is exactly what your restless soul needs.

Dear Lord, my soul is having a hard time being still. I lay down my resistance to silence, and commit to five minutes of daily silence with You for the next month. I praise You in advance for what You are going to say to me in the silence. Thank You for the rest only You can give. In Jesus' name, Amen.

REMEMBER

You are positioned to hear God most clearly when you are still and silent.

REFLECT

What concerns you and what intrigues you about being silent with God?

RESPOND

Commit to spending five minutes today in silence with God. Open your time of silence by praying Psalm 131:2. If you find it helpful, use a journal to briefly note observations about your time with God in silence.

POWER VERSES

Matthew 11:28 – 30; Ecclesiastes 3:7

For Our Greater Good

Micca Campbell

As for you, you meant evil against me,
but God meant it for good,
to bring it about that many people should be kept alive,
as they are today.
(GENESIS 50:20 ESV)

The Old Testament patriarch Joseph would have made a great talk show guest. I imagine the title of the program might have been something like *From the Pit to the Palace*.

Joseph deserved to be loved and nurtured by his parents. So did Joseph's brothers. But in the eyes of their father, Jacob, the brothers were second best to Joseph. Their father's rejection caused terrible sibling rivalry. Things got so bad that Joseph's brothers eventually threw him into a pit as a prelude to killing him.

While his brothers were eating supper and discussing how best to dispatch him, a caravan of Midianite traders en route to Egypt passed their camp. Seizing the opportunity, the brothers sold Joseph as a slave for twenty pieces of silver. In current monetary value, that's about $1.28.

Have you been rejected and thrown into the pit? Don't fear. God has not abandoned you. He knows your whereabouts. He is using your circumstance as a stepping-stone for a greater plan, just as He did for Joseph.

Seventeen years later, both the brothers and Joseph had experienced radical reversals. Joseph had risen to a position of power in Egypt and his brothers were rendered powerless by a life-threatening drought. When Joseph's brothers traveled to Egypt to buy grain, Joseph could have seized the opportunity to take revenge. Instead, he forgave his brothers and reunited with his family.

As his brothers bowed before Joseph in fear for their lives, he said, "As for you, you meant evil against me, but God meant it for good, to bring it about that many people should be kept alive, as they are today" (Genesis 50:20 ESV). This verse is often paired with the familiar words of the apostle Paul: "And we know that in all things God works for the good of those who love him, who have been called according to his purpose" (Romans 8:28).

When you and I let go of old hurts and trust God for the greater good, we find healing and restoration just as Joseph did. When we choose instead to cling to the pain, we get stuck in the pit and our wounds fester. God has so much more for us.

What was meant for evil, God wants to use for your good. The Lord wants to bring you out of the pit and place you in His palace. The choice is yours. Focus on bad experiences and miss out on joy; or, take the risk and forgive those who hurt you. God has a greater good in His plans for your future.

Dear Lord, Your promises sustain me and provide hope and peace while I'm in a pit. Help me trust in Your promises until You bring me out. In Jesus' name, Amen.

REMEMBER

What was meant for evil, God wants to use for your good.

REFLECT

Recall a benefit or two that you have reaped by allowing God to heal your hurts and bring restoration in a Joseph-like situation.

RESPOND

Practice shifting your perspective by reflecting on any evidence you can find that affirms God's grace and goodness in your life. Use a piece of paper or your journal to identify six to eight things you can affirm as God sustaining you and caring for you as He works for your greater good.

POWER VERSES

Psalm 18:30; Psalm 145:17

Mastering the Waves of Adversity

Tracie Miles

God is our refuge and strength, always ready to help in times
of trouble. So we will not fear when earthquakes come and
the mountains crumble into the sea. Let the oceans roar and foam.
Let the mountains tremble as the waters surge!

(PSALM 46:1–3 NLT)

My son and his friend made an excited dash toward the ocean with their inflated boat. Despite the gusty winds, they were determined to carry it to the water to ride on the waves. I watched as the raft flapped wildly in the air, nearly lifting the boys off the ground.

They made repeated efforts to get into the boat, but after being sucked under the rough waters multiple times, they finally admitted defeat. The waves had taken a toll on both their spirits and the raft, rendering both boys and boat helpless.

Watching their defenselessness against the whitecaps, I was reminded of a season when I felt powerless against the waves of adversity crashing against me. The economy was going downhill, severely affecting our family. My sister's chronic illness had gotten worse. One of my children faced a serious health issue. The washing machine broke, the transmission died, and a hailstorm damaged our roof. Each day seemed to bring with it a new tidal wave of problems, anxiety, and stress. It was a long season in which I felt sucked under by a raging current, barely able to hold my head above water. I was completely deflated, just like the boys' little raft.

During that time, I clung to the psalmist's wisdom about persevering through difficult times: "God is our refuge and strength … So we will not fear" (Psalm 46:1–2 NLT). This promise helped me to remember my need for God, and to rely on Him because I wasn't equipped to handle life on my own.

The truth is that none of us is equipped to handle life on our own. No matter how strong we think we are, there will come a time when the demands of life overwhelm us. We will desperately need a refuge from the storms and someone who understands what we're going through.

I understood the frustration of two little boys who wanted to ride the waves in their raft. After they rested and the wind lessened, they tried again and finally found themselves floating *in* the boat, instead of hanging from it.

God understands what we're going through. His Word promises He will help us in times of trouble. When adversity strikes, God offers Himself as our refuge and His strength to weather life's storms. No matter the problems tossing us about, we don't have to feel like we're simply hanging on. Instead, we can trust the One who offers us peace and carries us through until we get to calmer shores.

Dear Lord, I feel beaten down by the storms of life, drowning in a sea of adversity and stress. I commit to depend on You as my refuge and I place my trust in You. In Jesus' name, Amen.

REMEMBER

God is your refuge and true source of strength to handle life's adversities and storms.

REFLECT

Where have you been trying to manage life on your own instead of relying on God? What might be the benefit of learning to rely on His strength instead of your own?

RESPOND

Write down the most stressful circumstances you are juggling today. Surrender them to God in prayer, and ask Him to provide the strength and ability to trust Him in all things.

POWER VERSES

Psalm 9:9–10; Isaiah 41:10

When Friendship Is Tough

Lysa TerKeurst

Finally, all of you, be like-minded, be sympathetic,
love one another, be compassionate and humble.

(1 PETER 3:8)

One of the wisest pieces of advice on friendship I ever received was from one of my daughters. She was in middle school at the time. You know, that awkward place where insecurities run rampant, hormones rage, and your best friend one day becomes your worst enemy the next? So lovely.

She got into the car one day with tears filling her eyes. She waited until we pulled out of the school parking lot to let all her hurt leak down her cheeks.

"Rough day?" I asked.

"Awful," she replied.

I turned down the radio, waited until we were at a red light, and reached for her hand. "Wanna talk about it?"

"Nope," she whispered as she turned her face away from me toward the window. The rest of the night she sulked around the house. And no matter how many times I tried to get her to talk, this normally very talkative child wouldn't open up.

The next morning, I was surprised when she bounded down the stairs with a smile on her face.

"Well, hey! You sure look happy this morning," I said as I lifted up quick thank-you prayers to God for whatever had brought back the sunshine to my girl's life.

"Mom," she said with great authority, "I've decided something about friends. They all have good stuff and bad stuff. Things you like and things that really annoy you. So, you just have to decide if you can handle their package deal."

How wise. How true.

Friends are a package deal. And sadly, not all friendships will stand the test of time. Some friendships are for a season. But other times, we have to be willing to deal with the messy stuff to fight for our friendships.

31

Recently, I had something hard happen with a friend I dearly love and greatly respect. A misunderstanding. Hurt feelings. Frustration. Part of me wanted to distance myself because it was difficult to sift through the pain. But as I prayed through it, I had to remind myself this person is a package deal. Part of what makes her a great friend I love to be around is her tenacity and passion to accomplish tasks with excellence. But because she is so task oriented, she is less relationally sensitive.

And if I'm honest with myself, I can see that I'm a package deal too. With good stuff ... and annoying stuff.

She has issues. I have issues.

We're both messy people, willing to work on our not-so-fun stuff, fully aware we're going to hit some muddy little potholes along our friendship path.

But we've decided the package deal is worth it.

Dear Lord, thank You for my friendships. I know some will last a lifetime, and some will fade after a season. Please help me be completely humble and gentle, patient, bearing with my friends in love. In Jesus' name, Amen.

REMEMBER

Friends are a package deal. Not all friendships will stand the test of time. Some friendships are for a season; others we have to be willing to fight for.

REFLECT

What friendship have you let go of because it got messy? What do you think about fighting for this friendship and reestablishing it?

RESPOND

Consider one of your friends. How might you invest humility, gentleness, and patience in her or him today?

POWER VERSES

Ephesians 4:2–3; Colossians 3:13

Wait for Me

Lynn Cowell

He had no beauty or majesty to attract us to him,
nothing in his appearance that we should desire him.
(ISAIAH 53:2)

It was supposed to be a day of wonderful memories. The highlight of our trip would be Slippery Rock, a natural waterslide. However, following the guidance of a "local," we changed our plans to go to a different waterfall. When we reached that waterfall, we discovered it wasn't quite what we were told. The slide was steeper, there was less water, no lifeguard, no stairs, no rope. Though disappointed, we vowed to make the best of the situation.

From the bottom of the falls, Greg kept an eye on our kids as they climbed up the side of the steep hill and reached the top of the rock slide. He watched the older kids start their slide down the sheer slope. Sensing everything was not as smooth as it seemed, he called to our youngest daughter, Madison, "Wait for me. Let's go together and I will lead you."

Hearing Greg and the kids' laughter brought joy to my heart. Madison was safe in her daddy's lap as they began their descent down the natural rock slide into the chilly mountain water. But as I caught my husband's eye, I knew something was wrong. On the way down the hard slide, Greg extended his leg to avoid hitting a large boulder. He and Madison missed the boulder, but ended up in a spin that slammed them into the mountain wall — with Greg's bare back taking the blow.

Our fun day ended with a trip to the emergency room. The four-inch gash on Greg's back was evidence of how he had protected our daughter. Today, it's a thick red scar — proof of his love for his family.

The prophet Isaiah foretold Jesus' gruesome death ... and the source of His scars. "He had no beauty or majesty to attract us to him, nothing in his appearance that we should desire him" (Isaiah 53:2). Jesus' sacrificial death caused Him to bear scars of love ... proof that He protects.

As a young woman, my life path looked a lot like the uphill climb at the waterfall — no stairs, no rope, no lifeguard. I wanted to live a little, but the ride was more difficult than I'd anticipated. Just before I crashed, I listened to Jesus' invitation: *Wait for Me; let Me get you out of harm's way and lead you.* I fell into His accepting arms, rescued and safe. I was saved because of His death, which created the beautiful scars.

Many times we want to go our own way, oblivious to the dangers hidden just beneath the surface of selfish or sinful choices:

I can flirt with this sin; I just want a little fun!

It's my turn. My kids will bounce back.

I don't have to put up with him anymore. It's my life too.

Inevitable destruction follows. All along, Jesus calls out to us: *Wait for Me. Let's go together and I will lead you.*

In the exciting rush and roar of temptation, it's easy to disregard Jesus' invitation to wait. We refuse the strength that could rescue us. We overlook the scars—proof that His love held Him to a cross on our behalf.

Before we make our choices, we need to reflect on the cost He paid to protect us from our own destruction. It's truly a thing of love.

Dear Lord, help me look to You and trust Your instructions and warnings, knowing that You love me more than I love myself. You are my first love. In Jesus' name, Amen.

REMEMBER

Jesus' death and destruction have the power to keep you from your own death and destruction. Run toward that protection, not away from it.

REFLECT

In what areas of life are you most susceptible to flirting with something dangerous right now? What needs or wounds might be making you vulnerable to this temptation?

RESPOND

Take a moment to thank Jesus for a time when He saved you from something dangerous or destructive.

POWER VERSES

Isaiah 53:3–5; Psalm 18:6

If Only

T. Suzanne Eller

But godliness with contentment
is great gain.
(1 TIMOTHY 6:6)

Have you ever lived in the land of the if-onlys?

If only I had more money, things would be easier.

If only I lost ten pounds, I'd be happier.

If only they'd recognize my talent, I'd feel more appreciated.

Not too long ago, my husband and I were praying about his career. Not only did an answer not come, but every door shut that we thought would easily open. As time passed, I set up house in the land of my if-onlys.

If only we had clear direction.

If only we could begin that dream God placed in our hearts.

If only, if only, if only …

Soon these unspoken words dominated my thoughts. They crept into my prayers. They tiptoed into my relationship with my husband.

One day, while reading *King's Cross* by Timothy Keller, these words leapt from the page:

> The Bible says that our real problem is that every one of us is build-ing our identity on something besides Jesus. Whether it's to succeed in our chosen field or to have a certain relationship—or even to get up and walk—we're saying, "If I have that, if I get my deepest wish, then everything will be okay." …You've distorted your deepest wish by trying to make it into your savior.

I suddenly saw myself and how my deepest wish had shifted. Where once I longed for God, now my thoughts and actions revolved around what I didn't have and what I couldn't control.

That night I confessed to my husband that I had not only moved into the land of the if-onlys but had built a house and established citizenship there. I promised that instead of focusing on what we didn't have and what wasn't happening in our lives, I would begin to treasure what we did have.

Today we have food. We have shelter. Our home is warm. Thank You for that gift, Father.

Today I hold a grandbaby in my arms. See her precious smile? I delight in that, Lord.

Today I sit in the living room and laugh with my husband. Thank You for joy.

Today and every day I am Yours, Jesus. You are more than enough.

Godly contentment isn't passive but an active faith that says God is enough. You and I are okay because our deepest wish doesn't revolve around money in the bank, losing ten pounds, or being recognized for our efforts.

Are you living in the land of the if-onlys? If so, are you willing to change your deepest wish from the if-only to focusing instead on what you have and thanking God for it?

Dear Lord, I trust that You are enough and You are good. You are my sufficiency. I find my identity and joy in You. In Jesus' name, Amen.

REMEMBER

Don't miss the miracles of today because you are so focused on tomorrow.

REFLECT

Take a moment to consider your if-onlys. Write down one or two that come to mind. How much time and energy do you devote to thinking about these things or trying to make them happen?

RESPOND

For each if-only you identified, write down two or three statements that focus on treasuring what you *do* have. Use these statements to shift your perspective from the if-onlys to God.

POWER VERSES

Matthew 6:33–34; Hebrews 13:5

When Things Are Out of Our Hands

Samantha Evilsizer

I planted, Apollos watered,
but God was causing the growth.
(1 CORINTHIANS 3:6 NASB)

After several hours of mixing soil and hunching over garden beds, we arched our aching backs, brushed the smudges of soil from our arms, and surveyed our work. We had planted over two hundred seeds of twelve different vegetables. We had done everything we could. What those seeds did now — whether or not they grew — was out of our hands.

The hidden work of seeds is among the Bible's most vivid metaphors for spiritual growth. I was reminded of this recently when I received an email from an old friend.

Javier and I were neighbors in college. We spent lazy afternoons watching movies and cheering at football games. When I took guitar lessons, Javier taught me chords. We simply enjoyed hanging out together, but I'm sorry to say I rarely talked to him about my faith.

In the years since graduation, Javier and I have kept in touch sporadically, but I was amazed when I read this recent email from him:

> Sam, I wanted to thank you for being in my life in college. I came to Christ about four years ago. Lately, I've been looking back on my life and thinking of people who were examples I wanted to follow. Even though we hardly talked about God, I knew you were a Christian and really admired that about you. Talk about planting a seed that didn't bear fruit right away! I was *ten years* in the making. I am glad I am able to tell people like you how important they were in helping me to find Christ.

My heart leapt at his words. I never expected them. But the promise of Scripture is that if we're faithful to sow seeds into others, God will be faithful to nurture those seeds into a relationship with Him (1 Corinthians 3:6).

Have you prayed for a loved one's salvation? Or sought God's favor to restore your child, parent, spouse, or sibling to Him? Maybe you've planted every seed you can think of. Gotten on your knees. Shared verses. Given a Bible. Yet no sprout is appearing from the hard ground of your loved one's heart.

I wish I could say that I'd planted some intentional seeds with Javier: invited him to Bible study; welcomed him to prayer group; chosen the latest worship song to learn together on the guitar. These are wonderful ideas, but they weren't the seeds I planted. Instead, I simply lived out my daily relationship with Jesus. Some days my example was more stellar than others but, for better or worse, seeds were planted. Day by day, Javier saw me trusting, hoping, and finding joy in the Lord.

I don't know how much you've prayed, or what seeds you've planted. I do know this: when we faithfully plant seeds, the Lord honors that. He'll bring others around our loved one to water seeds we've sown. And most importantly, He'll make them grow. When the results are out of our hands, we can trust them in His.

Dear Lord, thank You for caring about my loved one's salvation. Please use me to plant seeds, bring others to water, and I trust that You will cause them to grow. In Jesus' name, Amen.

REMEMBER

When the results are out of our hands, we can trust them in His.

REFLECT

Why is it difficult to trust that a loved one will come to know the Lord?

RESPOND

Who in your life doesn't know the Lord? Plant a seed today by sharing a specific example of God's faithfulness in your own life and telling this person He can do the same in their life too.

POWER VERSES

Matthew 5:16; Romans 15:13

Don't Throw Away Your Confidence

Renee Swope

So do not throw away your confidence; it will be richly rewarded.
You need to persevere so that when you have done the will of God,
you will receive what he has promised.

(HEBREWS 10:35–36)

I was wiping down our kitchen countertops one afternoon when I found a little rubber thingy. I didn't know what it was, so I threw it away. But as soon as I tossed it into the trash can, I remembered it was the power button for our TV remote control.

Digging through layers of dirty paper plates, sticky plastic cups, and other stinky items, I finally found the tiny rubber button. As I retrieved it, I sensed God telling me that's how easily I throw away my confidence — without even recognizing what I'm doing.

Just hours earlier, I'd cried out to God from a place of agony and doubt, telling Him how impossible it was for me to finish a huge writing project. How stupid it was for me to commit to something I couldn't do. How much I hated the wide pendulum swings between my dreams and my realities.

As I stood there with the power button in my hand, I realized God was trying to show me what I had been throwing away for years. I was throwing away my confidence every time I said something like: *God, I can't do this. I'm not smart enough. My faith is too weak. My life is a mess. I'll never change.*

And every time I threw away my confidence, I threw away the power that could be mine if I chose to live in the security of God's promises instead of the insecurity of my doubts.

Do you ever question your abilities, your competency, or your worth? How often do you agree with the whispers of self-doubt and throw away confidence that should be yours as a child of God?

The next time you're tempted to throw away your confidence, ask God to help you throw away your insecurities instead.

When self-doubt whispers, *I can't do that. I'm going to fail and look foolish,* trash that lie and hold onto this truth: "The Lord is my helper; I will not be afraid. What can mere mortals do to me?" (Hebrews 13:6).

When self-doubt whispers, *I'll never change*, trash that lie and hold onto this truth: "For I am confident of this very thing, that He who began a good work in [me] will perfect it until the day of Christ Jesus" (Philippians 1:6 NASB).

When self-doubt whispers, *This is too hard for me. I don't have what it takes*, trash that lie and hold onto this truth: "No, in all these things [I am] more than [a conqueror] through him who loved [me]" (Romans 8:37).

Lord, help me recognize when I talk trash to myself and equip me to talk truth to my heart instead. I want to take hold of the power and security that is mine to live in through You. In Jesus' name, Amen.

REMEMBER

Every time you throw away your confidence, you throw away the power that could be yours if you chose to live in the security of God's promises instead of the insecurity of your doubts.

REFLECT

When does self-doubt most often rear its ugly head in your life?

RESPOND

Every time you think something doubtful today, write that thought down. For example, "I'll never be good enough to be promoted." "There is no way I will be loved." Now, crumple up your paper and throw it in the trash. Use one of the biblical promises from this devotion or another meaningful Scripture to replace the trash with truth.

POWER VERSES

Hebrews 10:39; Mark 9:23

Did I Really Say That?

Wendy Blight

A fool gives full vent to his anger,
but a wise man keeps himself under control.
(PROVERBS 29:11 NIV 1984)

I had just cleaned my kitchen—counters shining, stovetop sparkling, floors spotless. Within moments of completing this labor of love, my husband walked through the door. I should have been happy to see him, but I wasn't. He was going to create one of the gourmet sandwiches he loves. All I could think about was the mess he'd make, so I launched into a series of instructions:

"Please put your dishes in the dishwasher."

"Please wipe your crumbs off the counter."

"Please clean the stove I scrubbed."

I was polite. Did you count my "pleases"? I just have a way I like things to be done in my kitchen—*my* way.

The look on his face said what he was thinking: *You've got to be kidding! Why did I come home for lunch?*

I realized I was being nagging and controlling. This wasn't the first time.

Often after I speak such words, I find myself thinking, *Did I really just say that?*

When I make big deals out of minor things, resentment and discord inevitably follow. I recognize how damaging it can be, but sometimes it feels like I just can't help myself.

When I immerse myself in God's Word, I'm inspired to change. I promise myself that, no matter what—dishes in the sink, crumbs on the counter, grease on the stove—I won't say anything. But when the situation presents itself again, I blow it once more. Within minutes, the words start spewing.

I know I have a choice—I don't have to be this way. But then I hear that voice of justification: *It's just who I am.* But the truth is, it is *not* who

I am. It is who I'm *used to being*. It's not who God wants me to be. In fact, His Word tells me how my words should be:

Self-controlled: "A fool gives full vent to his anger, but a wise man keeps himself under control" (Proverbs 29:11 NIV 1984).

Edifying: "Do not let any unwholesome talk come out of your mouths, but only what is helpful for building others up according to their needs, that it may benefit those who listen" (Ephesians 4:29).

Gentle: "A gentle answer turns away wrath, but a harsh word stirs up anger" (Proverbs 15:1).

Compassionate: "Instead, be kind to each other, tenderhearted, forgiving one another, just as God through Christ has forgiven you" (Ephesians 4:32 NLT).

This is hard! Yet I believe God gives me strength through the power of His Holy Spirit. On days when I feel there's no way I can speak kindly, I try to remember I can do *all* things through Christ who strengthens me (Philippians 4:13).

When we quiet our hearts, when we open His Word instead of our mouths, when we submit to His ways ... that's when God does His work and helps us tame the tongue. And the next time we find ourselves thinking, "Did I really just say that?" let it be because we responded with patience, kindness, and gentleness.

Dear Lord, help me tame my tongue. Enable me through the power of Your Holy Spirit to speak gentle, edifying, self-controlled, compassionate words. In Jesus' name, Amen.

REMEMBER

You can choose the words you speak, and with Christ's help, you can speak gentle, edifying, self-controlled, compassionate words.

REFLECT

Draw a line down the center of a piece of paper. At the top of the left column, write "Life-Giving Words"; at the top of the right column, write "Life-Taking Words." Think back over the last twenty-four hours and write down three or four things you said that were life-giving; for example: expressing love, withholding an unnecessary comment, praising good work or behavior. Then write down three or four things you said that were life-taking; for example: lying, complaining, and criticizing. What do your two lists reveal about how you use words?

RESPOND

Identify one relationship in which you can invest life-giving words today. Write down two or three things you could say to bring life to this person with your words.

POWER VERSES

Proverbs 12:18; Ephesians 4:32

The Moment

Lysa TerKeurst

And yet I will show you the most excellent way.
If I speak in the tongues of men or of angels, but do not have love,
I am only a resounding gong or a clanging cymbal.
(1 CORINTHIANS 12:31 – 13:1)

Each morning, I have a routine with my man. It's simple. Nothing profound. Nothing for which we'd ever stop and snap a picture.

It's just a moment.

He asks me to help him pick a tie. He then goes away to fuss with this fixture of his professional job. Soon, he returns with a flipped up collar and a pressed down, knotted tie. He needs gentle hands to fold the collar over. Actually, he doesn't *need*. He *wants* gentle hands to fold the collar over.

And I do.

It's just a moment.

But it's a moment when we follow the "excellent way" of love. In the intersection of this moment, we're once again saying to each other: *I love you; I love you too.*

Now, please don't get an overly idyllic picture in your head of our marriage. Heavens, no. We have plenty of those "growth opportunity" moments too.

But this moment with the tie, it's like a spot of glue ever tightening the bond between us day by day. It's so simple, and yet something I would miss with the deepest ache imaginable if today were the last of the moments.

If today.

Tears slip as I think about this. *Dear God, help me think about this.* Let me snap a hundred of these moments with the lens of my heart to be stored and appreciated and thought of as the great treasures they are.

Let my mind park there.

Let my heart relish there.

Let my mouth dare to whisper what a joy this is. *I love you. I love us. I love this moment each day.*

Our relationship isn't perfect; no relationship is perfect. We're two very strong-willed people with vastly different approaches to life. And, oh, how easy it would be to list all the differences. He likes the towel hanging in the same spot. I am more creative. But I stop the list there.

I stop because great love isn't two people finding the perfect match in one another. Great love is two people making the choice to be a match. A decision. To fold his collar and snap the heart lens and find myself grateful to the point of tears. Tears of relishing today are so much better than tears of what was missed.

It's just a moment.

Or is it?

Dear Lord, help me to appreciate each moment given to me. I want to park my mind on the daily moments I too often take for granted. Thank You for this joy, so simple but so sweet. In Jesus' name, Amen.

REMEMBER

Let me snap a hundred "I love you" moments with the lens of my heart to be stored and appreciated and thought of as the great treasures they are.

REFLECT

In what ways can you turn everyday moments into treasures? It may be as simple as relishing a moment in your heart or it may mean beginning a new moment every day, such as folding a collar over a necktie.

RESPOND

Discuss your "moments" with your spouse, your family, or a friend. Ask what stands out to them as important and meaningful and choose together to relish them. Take a photograph or journal about one moment.

POWER VERSES

1 Peter 4:8; Psalm 90:12

Making the Most of Loneliness

Glynnis Whitwer

*"I no longer call you servants, because a servant does not know
his master's business. Instead, I have called you friends, for everything
that I learned from my Father I have made known to you."*
(JOHN 15:15)

My little son sat looking out the front window. His head resting on crossed arms, he watched two neighbor boys race past on bikes.

I watched Joshua from the kitchen door, drying my hands with a dish towel. My shoulders drooped as he let out a despairing sigh. Mirroring his sadness, hot tears burned my eyes. Setting the towel on the counter, I quietly sat down next to him. Without saying a word, I scooped him into my lap and enveloped his little frame with my arms.

His face nuzzled mine and our tears mixed together. I could almost feel the wishing and hoping pulse through his small body: *Will they stop by* my *house? Will they invite* me *to play?* A smothered sob escaped from my little boy, who was trying valiantly to be "big."

Ever since our move earlier in the year, Joshua had had trouble making friends. The local playgroups were already established, and my shy son was painfully left on the outside. His little brothers were good companions at home, but that didn't replace friendships at school or in the neighborhood.

The loneliness was oppressive, and I felt it too. In fact, that period of my life was one of my darkest times. We had all left lifelong friends when we moved. Those friendships had been born of common experiences and years spent together. They were effortless.

Now we faced unknown territory, not just geographically, but culturally and socially. This was a new world to us, and Josh felt it as painfully as I did. And yet, during that time, God used loneliness to teach us things we couldn't learn when our lives were filled with friends.

I learned there are times when God uses loneliness as an invitation. He invites us to turn to Him for advice, to seek His comfort, and to pursue Him as our closest friend. In our pain, God reveals His presence in new ways.

God longs to fill our lonely hearts with Himself. Yet, we often try to fill the desires of our hearts with the things of this world. However, those attempts to find replacements for God are fleeting and insubstantial, leaving us even lonelier than before.

As you face a time of loneliness, take this opportunity to look to Jesus as a best friend. Jesus said: "I have called you friends, for everything that I learned from my Father I have made known to you" (John 15:15).

Even though we were designed for community, God has a purpose for loneliness. If we can learn from it, rather than run from it or resent it, we'll find a lifelong Friend who'll never leave us lonely.

Dear Lord, thank You for being a friend who will never leave me.
Sometimes the loneliness is overwhelming. Please be real to me today.
I want to learn from this time of loneliness rather than run from it
or resent it. In Jesus' name, Amen.

REMEMBER

Sometimes God uses loneliness as an invitation to pursue Him as our closest friend.

REFLECT

In what ways would you say Jesus has revealed Himself to you as a friend?

RESPOND

Take a moment to consider what it means to be a good friend. Write down three or four things that come to mind. Using these characteristics as a reference, identify one way you might be a better friend to God today.

POWER VERSES

James 2:23; Joshua 1:5

Unfolding

Amy Carroll

May the favor of the Lord our God rest on us;
establish the work of our hands for us—
yes, establish the work of our hands.

(PSALM 90:17)

I stared into the frustrated eyes of my friend last week as we talked about her calling to write. She has big, big dreams, and her dreams seem to be taking far too long to come true. I told her how much I understood. Stepping into my calling was a long time coming too.

My calling is to teach, speak, and write. Your calling may fall into a myriad of other categories, but every calling is equally high when it's lived out in obedience to the Most High. We are *all* called to ministry.

My calling didn't materialize in a year or even two. It has unfolded during the last thirty-five years, and each phase of that unfolding has shaped and changed me. The unfolding progressed something like this:

- I became a passionate teacher of young children.
- I married my best friend.
- I invested years in my little boys' lives.
- I taught adults as they chased dreams that had passed them by in their teens.
- I volunteered in a women's ministry.
- I visited home after home as the "Welcome Wagon Lady" in my town.
- I accepted invitations to speak at my church and other churches close by.
- I joined the Proverbs 31 Ministries' speaker team.
- I returned to a frustrating year of elementary school teaching.
- I stepped into my calling of equipping others in their calling.

I've looked at this list many times and thought, *Wow. I wasted a lot of years to finally discover my calling.* But I've come to realize that's just not true. Every relationship, every job, every opportunity has prepared me for what

I'm doing now. The psalmist reminds me that God establishes the work of my hands. Each change presented me with an invitation to view that next place as a stepping-stone into a calling. Sometimes I accepted the invitation, and sometimes I didn't.

I was often irritated at the apparent meaninglessness of what I was doing, but now I see the significance of each stepping-stone. Every diaper changed, every knee kissed, every book read, every late-night listening session, every choice to die to self, every lesson plan, every story, every presentation, every meeting, every spreadsheet, *every thing* ...

It all counted.

Every moment was an unfolding of my eventual calling. God used each stepping-stone to establish me in the work I'm doing now.

Don't despair today if you can't see it. Obey God and trust that He is working. His timing is so rarely ours, but it is always perfect. Instead of chafing under the seemingly mundane, embrace each task as a building block for the dreams in your heart. Don't give up hope.

I promise, it's coming.

Dear Lord, it's been difficult waiting to step into my calling as the years have come and gone. Please help me appreciate each seemingly mundane task and day as a means to You establishing the work of my hands. In Jesus' name, Amen.

REMEMBER

Every moment is an unfolding of your eventual calling.

REFLECT

What periods of your life did you once consider wasted that you now see as fruitful times of training?

RESPOND

Write down four to six things you might consider among the more "mundane" things required of you in this season of your life. How do you imagine God might be using them to establish the work of your hands?

POWER VERSES

Romans 11:33–36; 1 Peter 4:10–11

Coming Back

Luann Prater

" 'Father, I have sinned against heaven and before you.
I am no longer worthy to be called your son.
Treat me as one of your hired servants.' "
(LUKE15:18 – 19 ESV)

Kay was a prodigal. She had been stunningly beautiful, but now her beauty was hollow and worn. Downcast with shoulders slumped, she walked through the doors of her childhood church.

Heads turned and whispers followed her as she made her way to the front of the church during an invitation to come forward for prayer. She fell to her knees at the altar. A group gathered around her and prayed for what seemed like an eternity. She slowly rose to her feet and was asked, "Did you pray through?" to which the weary wanderer replied, "I think so."

I don't remember seeing Kay back in church again.

In my church, the phrase "pray through" was synonymous with striving, straining, and working to find grace and deliverance. When I became a prodigal myself and wanted desperately to find answers and deliverance, I remembered Kay's forlorn look and decided to keep wandering. It just seemed easier than trying to "pray through."

Have you been wandering, looking for answers? Do you long to return to the Father after being far away but hesitate, wondering how you will make it back to Him and what it will cost you?

When coming "back home" we often have the same mentality as the prodigal son (Luke 15:18 – 19). Feeling worn down and unworthy, we come to our Father thinking we have to work like hired servants to earn our place.

After many years, I discovered that forgiveness and salvation aren't chores for us to labor over. They are free gifts from an amazing God! Jesus offers these gifts to all who believe in His name.

Jesus says, "Come to me." Period. It really isn't any more complicated than that. He loves you. He has been waiting for you and He welcomes you with open arms. We don't have to work for forgiveness or "pray through" like those well-meaning people in my childhood church felt the need to do.

God's heart for us is the same as the father's heart for his prodigal son: "But while [the prodigal son] was still a long way off, his father saw him and was filled with compassion for him; he ran to his son, threw his arms around him and kissed him" (Luke 15:20).

When you come to Jesus, when you allow Him to walk through the door of your heart, no pleading or striving is necessary; you need only believe that His salvation and grace are His gifts for you. No need to "pray through." He is watching for you, eager to throw His arms of love and compassion around you.

Dear Lord, thank You for giving us the gift of salvation through Jesus. I ask You to come into my heart and forgive me. Help me live in the freedom that You promise. In Jesus' name, Amen.

REMEMBER

Jesus says, "Come to me." Period. It really isn't any more complicated than that. He loves you. He has been waiting for you, and He welcomes you with open arms.

REFLECT

In what large or small ways have you wandered away from home or determined to go your own way? What keeps you from returning to the Father?

RESPOND

Is there a "prodigal" in your life? How might you show this person unconditional love this week?

POWER VERSES

John 6:37; Hebrews 10:22

In the Midst of Dirty Dishes

Sharon Glasgow

*Show hospitality to one another without grumbling. As each has received
a gift, use it to serve one another, as good stewards of God's varied grace:
. . . whoever serves, as one who serves by the strength that God supplies—
in order that in everything God may be glorified through Jesus Christ.*

(1 PETER 4:9–11 ESV)

She and her husband had been missionaries for over sixty years and led
countless people to Christ. Now she was in her eighties and still serving.
My friend Sheli and I were honored to stay with her for a week to minister alongside her.

After traveling thirty hours to her home in Takamatsu, Japan, we
arrived late in the evening. She ushered us into her kitchen for a hearty
meal, then prayed for us before we all went to bed. When the sun was
barely up the next morning, we feasted on an enormous breakfast in her
tiny kitchen.

The kitchen was crowded, her appliances old and worn, dishes piled
high in the sink from her lavish food preparation—yet the atmosphere
felt entirely like *home*. As she and her husband read Scripture and encouraged us, tears welled up in my eyes, the love of Christ enveloped us; it
overwhelmed me.

Immediately after breakfast, she began cooking again, this time for 100
women. She'd rented a banquet hall and invited friends, telling them an
American would be speaking and there would be food. We cooked, set
up tables for the luncheon, and then I was ushered to the front to speak.
Her objective in hosting the event was to build a bridge in hopes that
those who came for lunch would come back again for church on Sunday.
Many did!

While driving home after the lunch, she told me she'd invited a large
group to the house for dinner that night. I couldn't imagine how we could
clean up the mess we'd left behind and simultaneously prepare another
meal. How would we get it all done? She didn't seem concerned. Instead,
she was fueled by the energy of what the Lord had done at the luncheon.

There have been times I've worried more about my kitchen than how I can serve others. I fret over the size and messiness. But I was inspired as I watched this woman who had no concerns about the dirty pots in her sink. She didn't let an unswept floor keep her from ministering. She set the table beautifully and welcomed her guests. She and her husband prayed and read Scripture. Hearts melted.

Years have passed since that week in Japan and I think of this woman whenever I have company. Over her lifetime, she has ministered to thousands in her home, and many have come to know Jesus there. Her ministry has nothing to do with a spotless kitchen. In fact, her kitchen was a mess. But whenever God opens a window of opportunity, she seizes it.

I want my service to be like that described by the apostle Peter, grounded in "the strength that God supplies." I want to long for people to know Jesus more than I long for the perfect kitchen.

God cares more about what's happening among the people in our kitchen than He cares about the state of it. My missionary friend taught me that it is possible to share God's love, demonstrate His character, and offer hospitality, even in the midst of dirty dishes.

Dear Lord, show me ways to serve through the resources You've given me. Help me care more about people than things like dirty dishes. In Jesus' name, Amen.

REMEMBER

Your kitchen is a perfect place to show hospitality. Don't wait for it to be perfect to invite guests. God will supply the ability you need to minister in your kitchen, and He will be glorified.

REFLECT

Would you be willing to invite people to stay for dinner if they dropped by unannounced—even if your kitchen was a mess? Why or why not?

RESPOND

Can you think of a person, family, or neighbor who doesn't know Jesus that you could invite for dinner? Make a call and get it on the calendar.

POWER VERSES

Proverbs 31:15; Proverbs 31:25–27

Easy Isn't the New Good

Lysa TerKeurst

He has shown you, O mortal, what is good.
And what does the LORD require of you?
To act justly and to love mercy and to walk humbly with your God.

(MICAH 6:8)

It's good to invest wisely in my relationships. It's easy to simply coast.

It's good to go the speed limit. It's easy to speed a little.

It's good to make a healthy choice. It's easy to grab junk.

It's good to read my Bible. It's easy to check my phone for texts and emails first.

It's good to think about others. It's easy to think about myself.

Several years ago, I had a friend who decided to leave her husband for another man. Things were easier with this other man. The feelings were giddy. The fights were few. And they didn't have years of issues that needed to be dealt with.

So she went with what felt easy over what was good. She divorced. She remarried. She started over with what seemed so much easier.

The truth is, she'd been slipping into the pattern of choosing easy for years. When we set our hearts on the pattern of choosing easy over good in the little things, we run the risk of using the same justifications with the bigger things.

I'm not saying if I don't read my Bible today, I'm headed for divorce court tomorrow. But setting a pattern of choosing easy over good in my life is a slippery slope.

Easy isn't the new good.

Just because the world waves a big banner that we deserve easy—*Do what feels easy. Why stress yourself when there's an easier way?*—doesn't mean it's good.

Eventually, my friend didn't feel like her new man was so easy. The feelings weren't so giddy. The fights were many. And over the years they too developed a whole host of issues. One day she came home and her second husband was gone. He found it easy to leave.

Like the old cliché says, "Easy come, easy go."

I think about this and I'm challenged. Where are little compromises sneaking into my life? Where am I establishing a pattern of choosing what is easy over what is good? And does it really matter?

I think it does.

"He has shown you, O mortal, what is good. And what does the LORD require of you? To act justly and to love mercy and to walk humbly with your God" (Micah 6:8).

I so desire this good way. To treat others fairly. To love those in my life faithfully. And to live the way God wants me to live — choosing good over easy.

Dear Lord, please help me to see today the times when I may choose the easy way over the good way. My desire is to please You in all that I do. Help me to establish healthy patterns of living according to Your purpose. In Jesus' name, Amen.

REMEMBER

Just because the world waves a big banner that we deserve easy, that doesn't mean it's good.

REFLECT

Are there little compromises sneaking into your life? Where are you choosing what is easy over what is good?

RESPOND

Call a trusted friend today and confess to her areas you have chosen easy over good. Ask her to hold you accountable to not compromising.

POWER VERSES

Romans 8:28; Philippians 2:13

Emptying and Filling My Nest

Van Walton

For there is a proper time and procedure for every matter,
though a person may be weighed down by misery.
(ECCLESIASTES 8:6)

This spring, I watched two cardinals build a nest, nurture their eggs, and feed their young. Then one day, with an encouraging chirp, the mom and dad nudged their three tiny offspring out of the only home they'd ever known. Their empty nest brought pain to my heart as I reflected on the emptiness of my own home.

Memories of times gone by brought extreme sadness. With my children grown and gone, I felt an acute loss of purpose that often led to tears. The silence in the house felt like a crushing weight.

Now what?

I thought I could just get over it, ignore it, or talk myself back to life as usual. I could not. Eventually, I sought the help of a counselor to address my paralyzing empty-nest sadness.

My counselor asked about my passions and joys. "Your dreams have all come true. Your sons graduated, left home, and are living the independent lives you prepared them for." He also reminded me that I hadn't changed. I still had the same talents and gifts I'd used in raising my kids, but now I could focus them in a new direction. I realized I had a choice: I could concentrate on my perceived losses, or I could center my attention on God's purpose for this new season in my life. The words of Ecclesiastes offered me new hope: "There's a right time for everything on the earth ... a right time to hold on and another to let go" (Ecclesiastes 3:1, 6 MSG).

I felt God's affirmation that I had been a good mother: "Well done ... You have been faithful in handling this small amount, so now I will give you many more responsibilities" (Matthew 25:23 NLT).

And I sensed God's encouragement to step out and use what I'd learned as a mother to help others: "She extends her hand to the poor, and she stretches out her hands to the needy ... Strength and dignity are her clothing, and she smiles at the future. She opens her mouth in wisdom,

56

and the teaching of kindness is on her tongue" (Proverbs 31:20, 25–26 NASB).

As mothers, we move through different seasons of life. Even when our children are grown, there are always people who need our love and talents. The invitation of each new season is to ask God to show us the next step in His plan for our lives.

Dear Lord, please guide me to new opportunities. Remind me to celebrate the past and smile at the future. In Jesus' name, Amen.

REMEMBER

Choose to look forward, not backward.

REFLECT

How has focusing on what you miss from days gone by hurt you and others?

RESPOND

Research nonprofit organizations in your community where you can give of yourself to others. Make a phone call and set up a time for a get-acquainted visit. You may find your passion being ignited the minute you walk through the doors.

POWER VERSES

Ecclesiastes 3:1, 3–4; Psalm 138:8

Listening to God

Renee Swope

So Jesus explained, "I tell you the truth,
the Son can do nothing by himself.
He does only what he sees the Father doing.
Whatever the Father does, the Son also does."

(JOHN 5:19 NLT)

I want to be a woman who listens to God. But sometimes I'm not sure if it's God talking or just me thinking. And if I'm really honest, when I do sense Him whispering to my heart, I'm not always crazy about what I think He's asking me to do. Like the time I knew God wanted me to share my testimony publicly. I pretty much ran from that assignment for a decade.

Yet, I learned over time that when I listen to God, I discover His best for me and my trust in Him grows. At the end of my ten-year sprint away from what scared me most — sharing the story of my brokenness with others — I surrendered to what God was calling me to do. And I started listening closely *to* Him and trusting completely *in* Him.

Honestly, I thought I had been listening to Him all along. But one day while I was seeking God's direction in some decisions, the Holy Spirit showed me I had a habit of asking God what He was calling me to, and then went about doing it without depending on Him for direction each step of the way. I sought God for the larger plans in life, convinced that if I figured out what He wanted me to do, I could take it from there.

Perhaps you've had similar thoughts: If God would show me what job to take; what man to marry; what church to attend; what ministry to serve in — then my life would be complete and I'd trust Him with my whole heart. The problem is, sometimes we get a glimpse of where God wants us to go and then assume we know how to get there on our own. How many times have I made that mistake and wondered why I wasn't getting anywhere?

Over time, God has taught me that He wants my spiritual ears more than my spiritual efforts. He wants daily dependence, interaction, and intimacy with me. And He is more concerned with my character than what I schedule for Him on my calendar.

Jesus depended on the Father for the large and fine print of His life plan. He listened closely and obeyed quickly: "I tell you the truth, the Son can do nothing by himself. He does only what he sees the Father doing. Whatever the Father does, the Son also does" (John 5:19 NLT).

Like Jesus, we will discover God's purpose for our lives through dependent hearts that seek to listen to His—day by day, moment by moment. Let's position our hearts, minds, and souls to hear Him speak to us today.

Dear Lord, I want to become a woman who listens to You. I come to You today with a seeking heart, asking not only for direction but for discernment, humility, and dependence on You—each step of the way. In Jesus' name, Amen.

REMEMBER

Listen for God's voice not only to discover where He wants you to go, but also how He wants you to get there.

REFLECT

What holds you back the most from really listening to God? Past experiences? Fear? Time? Navigate through these to clear a path to hear from Him.

RESPOND

Take a look at your schedule for this week so far. How much time have you spent talking to friends and family (or even yourself!) versus time you've spent reading the Bible and praying? Commit to fifteen undivided minutes with God by the end of today.

POWER VERSES

Psalm 119:16; 1 Samuel 3:10

Exploding

Melissa Taylor

Do not let any unwholesome talk come out of your mouths,
but only what is helpful for building others up according to their needs,
that it may benefit those who listen.
(EPHESIANS 4:29)

I was in shock as I watched the explosion of anger on the field. A man was screaming rude and venomous words—words you don't want your child to hear. When the Little League umpire made a game-deciding call the coach didn't like, the coach made sure everyone knew how much he disagreed. He got in the umpire's face expressing his irate opinion in no uncertain terms. To drive home his point, he marched across the field to the opposing team's coach and shouted in his face too. This man had come completely unglued, spewing his anger on everyone around him.

The coach's lack of self-control and harsh words brought down two teams of Little Leaguers, their parents, and the officials. His uncontrolled explosion caused a ripple effect that ruined what should have been a great day for many people.

Maybe you've been caught in the path of an exploder too. One minute you're at a happy family gathering and before you know it, a feud between your uncle and cousin escalates into a shouting match. One of them storms out, everyone else is stressed out and sad, and the day is ruined.

Perhaps you're at work ready to tackle the day, only to be met by a disgruntled boss. He barks a few negative words and suddenly you are left walking on eggshells.

It could be that the explosive actions that make you tense are from someone closer—a spouse or a child. Or maybe the harsh behavior is coming from ... you.

The teaching of Scripture is that we are to use our words to build others up. We are to "get rid of all bitterness, rage and anger, brawling and slander, along with every form of malice" (Ephesians 4:31). Yet, too often we react before considering this truth or a better response.

Sometimes curbing our anger and choosing calm words isn't what we want to do, or at times even feel capable of doing. Whether we are on the receiving end of the explosion or the giving end, we have a choice of what words and tone we use.

God's Word encourages us to respond with grace and self-control. By doing this, not only will our lives have less stress and more peace, but we will build up instead of tear down those around us.

Dear Lord, help me think about how my words and actions affect those around me. I want to honor You in all I say and do. In Jesus' name, Amen.

REMEMBER

You have a choice of what words and tone you use when responding to others.

REFLECT

How can you apply Ephesians 4:31 to your life today?

RESPOND

For the next twenty-four hours, fast from angry (explosive) words. When confronted with a person or situation that pushes your buttons, curb your anger and choose calm words.

POWER VERSES

Ephesians 4:31; Proverbs 15:1

Battle in the Night

Lynn Cowell

By day the LORD directs his love,
at night his song is with me—
a prayer to the God of my life.

(PSALM 42:8)

How could this have happened? What could I have done to stop it?

One of my kids had made a decision that sent my emotions into a tailspin and another sleepless night was upon me; my mind wouldn't shut off. During the day I had managed to focus on God's promise to make all things work together for good. But as day faded into night, the struggle to trust became more than I could take.

Many nights as I lie in bed, my mind pulls me into a downward spiral of focusing on my troubles. It's then and there that the battle is most intense. A war wages between my faith and fears.

What if my loved one never knows Jesus?

Will my kids make the right choices with their peers?

What can I do for my friend who struggles with cancer?

Even though my body is still, my thoughts are at war.

Do you struggle in the quiet of the night? Maybe you have thoughts like these: *Nobody else has troubles. Other people are just enjoying their lives. Why is mine so hard?* The battles we face are real, and rob us of joy as well as sleep.

This is why I love King David's encouraging words in Psalm 42. During the day he allowed the Lord's love to direct him. Knowing he was loved gave him the strength to make the hard choices that were the best choices. At night he put away all the words and hard thinking and devoted himself to praising God.

I want to do the same. When the lights are turned out, I want to choose a song of praise, arming myself with truth and worship for the only One who can carry and fix my troubles. When my mind tries to take a turn and go around that problem one more time, I want to make the choice to stop and sing (even if only in my head).

I gave this a try the other night while stewing over my worries. It reminded me of a sign my mom has in her home: "Give me all your troubles before you go to bed. I'm going to be up anyway."—God

Pick a song you can sing at night when trouble comes knocking and worry wants to run rampant in your heart and mind. Make your prayer a song to God and choose a song of praise to sing to Him all day long—from sunrise to late in the evening. Watch your heart go from fear to faith as you trust in the Lord.

Dear Lord, I feel stronger in the day than in the night. Bring to mind a song of praise I can sing that will lift my thoughts and strengthen my faith in You. In Jesus' name, Amen.

REMEMBER

When you are tired and quiet at night, you can be more susceptible to runaway emotions. You can guard your heart from fear by singing praises to your King as your mind and body find their rest.

REFLECT

Think about what song you would choose as your song of praise.

RESPOND

Write down Psalm 42:8, and put it next to your bed to remind you to look to the Lord as you go to sleep.

POWER VERSES

Psalm 94:18–19; Exodus 15:2

Broken Places

T. Suzanne Eller

We now have this light shining in our hearts,
but we ourselves are like fragile clay jars
containing this great treasure.
(2 CORINTHIANS 4:7 NLT)

I knew Shana had secrets. I pressed gently, but she shied away. I prayed she would tell me when she was ready.

The phone call finally came.

"Can you come get me?"

When I arrived, I found her battered, and we drove to get medical help. She spilled her secrets on the way. Her mother was often beaten. She and her siblings were secondary targets. Leaving home had been her only escape. She had returned to visit, only to find her brother being abused. She stepped in and crushing blows followed. Her father only stopped when she begged for her life.

Shana came to live with us until she found a safer environment. In those two months, we often stayed up late talking. Her greatest fear was that she would always feel broken.

The apostle Paul also knew what it was to be bruised and battered. He was wrongly imprisoned and beaten—multiple times. He once described himself as a chipped clay jar, saying, "We get knocked down, but we are not destroyed" (2 Corinthians 4:9 NLT). Paul had discovered something valuable. There was a light inside that fractured jar healing the hurting places on the interior, then shining through the broken places so the world could see.

That treasure, nestled in the center of the clay, was Jesus.

As time passed, Shana began to see herself through that light. She wasn't just a battered daughter; she was a woman with purpose. The wounds inflicted by her earthly father took time to heal, but as they did, she was led to share her story. Her message is this:

You are loved.

You are made for more than this.

God can and will heal the broken parts of your heart.

Today Shana is a mom and a wife. The treasure inside this woman illuminates through the once-broken places in a powerful way. She has adopted a son and fostered other children who came to her home with their own broken places, hoping to love them into wholeness. Children trust her because she understands their pain, but also because of the light and love they see inside her.

Maybe you were bruised by an earthly parent's words or actions. May I tell you something? Those words, those actions, do not define you.

There are thousands, like Shana, like me, who were once chipped and broken. God blazed His light through our cracks, not just healing us, but allowing His light to lead others into His loving arms.

God sees you. He loves you. He's reaching out to make you whole again.

Dear Lord, I can't change what happened to me, but I can open my heart to the treasure of You. You are the light in my darkness. Heal my brokenness from the inside out. In Jesus' name, Amen.

REMEMBER

Consider a piece of mosaic art. Such vivid colors. Such startling patterns. A pile of broken tiles, when placed in the Master's hand, becomes a new creation. God can make your broken places whole.

REFLECT

In what ways has God already taken your broken pieces and made them beautiful?

RESPOND

Read Ephesians 1:18. Make this paraphrased Scripture your prayer today: *I pray that my heart will be flooded with light so that I can understand the confident hope Christ has given to me, for He has called me as His own to a rich and glorious inheritance.*

POWER VERSES

Psalm 147:3; Psalm 34:18

I Gotta Die

Karen Ehman

*[I assure you] by the pride which I have in you
in [your fellowship and union with] Christ Jesus our Lord,
that I die daily [I face death every day and die to self].*
(1 CORINTHIANS 15:31 AMP)

My son has a fondness for iPod games where a creature has to jump and dart in an effort to stay alive. Often he plays them on our commute to school. As we drive, we review the pick-up instructions for that day: at the middle school after wrestling practice? Or at the high school if there is weight lifting that day? The man cub just keeps playing his game, acting as if he's not listening. But I know he is.

When we pull up in the carpool line, I inform my boy it's time to get out of the vehicle. Usually, still engaged in the game, he mutters something like, "Hang on a second, I gotta die." In other words, *I'm still finishing this level. Let my character finish this level until it dies. Then I'll get out of the car.* When he said it this morning, it spoke to my soul.

As a follower of Christ, I am to die to self. But too often, I do not. Instead, I elevate self. I promote self. I think little of the other person and much of me. But before I react, before I hurl a harsh word, pass judgment, speak unkindly to my husband, or snap at my child, perhaps I need to take a deep breath. To pause and ponder. To say in a spiritual sense, *Hang on a second, I gotta die.*

Die to self.

Die to flesh.

Die to my "rights" that often result in my acting wrongly.

Yes, Paul said it best in 1 Corinthians 15: "I die daily."

Does this mean in *everything*?

When we think of Jesus' admonition that there is no greater love than to lay down your life for a friend, we may think of the dramatic ways that might happen. We might jump in front of a car to get our friend out of harm's way. Soldiers might willingly give up their lives on the battlefield.

But what if it also means that we learn to die to self in the everyday details of life? In our interactions with others, especially our own families?

These daily, hourly, and even moment-by-moment decisions are difficult! And, if we're trying to make them in our own strength, they will also be impossible. It's at these junctures we must draw deep from the power the Holy Spirit offers and let His graced response override our sinful one.

So, the next time you want to react in a way that won't please God, remember my game-lovin' son. And *before* you speak, take a deep breath — a pause that centers your heart, snaps your soul to attention, and declares, *Hang on a second, I gotta die.*

Dear Lord, may I purpose to die daily, to both act and react in ways that please You. In Jesus' name, Amen.

REMEMBER

When we die to ourselves, we are more able to live effectively for Christ and to love others.

REFLECT

How often do you put yourself first and then interact with others in a way that is not God honoring? The next time you feel unkind words or actions surfacing, what can you do to make your interactions with others pleasant and peaceful as you remember the concept of dying to self?

RESPOND

When you are about to say or do something selfish, repeat silently in your mind the phrase, "Hang on a second, I gotta die." To aid you in making dying to self your aim, write that phrase on sticky notes and post them in prominent places where you will see them throughout your day.

POWER VERSES

Romans 2:7–8; Philippians 2:3–4

Just a Little Sin?

Lysa TerKeurst

Joseph went after his brothers and found them near Dothan.
But they saw him in the distance, and before he reached them,
they plotted to kill him.

(GENESIS 37:17 – 18)

Today there will be a moment. No one will snap a picture of it. It probably won't make it into a daily journal entry or linger in the thoughts we carry to sleep tonight.

It will come.

It will go.

It will slip by seemingly unnoticed. But its effects will stay. And if fostered, it will grow to epic proportions.

This is the moment when something creeps into our hearts and pulls our focus from right to wrong. It will be just a hint of distortion. But a seemingly insignificant amount of skewed thought will take root.

And grow.

Remember in the Bible where Moses goes to Pharaoh and sings, "O Pharaoh, Pharaoh, whoa ohhh, gotta let my people go"? Okay, that's totally a loose translation, but here's an astounding chain of events to consider. Why was the entire nation of Israelites enslaved in Egypt? Trace this story backward and you'll find it's because of one moment: when the brothers of one family got jealous of their younger sibling, Joseph. Envy and anger slipped in. Just a hint. But just enough.

Joseph was thrown into a pit and eventually sold as a slave. Years of heartbreak and confusion followed.

Eventually, Joseph rose to a position of great power in Egypt and had authority to provide food for his family. His brothers and their families moved to Egypt. Those families became twelve tribes and as those tribes multiplied, they became the nation of Israel.

What the brothers meant for evil, God used for good (Genesis 50:20). He saved the Israelites from the famine. But there were still lasting effects of the brothers' choices that came out years later. After Joseph died ...

A new king, to whom Joseph meant nothing, came to power in Egypt. "Look," he said to his people, "the Israelites have become far too numerous for us. Come, we must deal shrewdly with them or they will become even more numerous and, if war breaks out, will join our enemies, fight against us and leave the country." So they put slave masters over them to oppress them with forced labor, and they built Pithom and Rameses as store cities for Pharaoh (Exodus 1:8–11).

So, the entire nation of Israel suffered oppression and slavery. Why? Because a few brothers got a little jealous and allowed anger to slip in. And the moment it slipped in, the course of history was forever changed.

May we never assume our moments don't matter. The decisions we make every second of every day matter. So, we fall hard upon soft grace. And ask God to make us more sensitive, more aware, more in tune to our constant need for forgiveness.

Watch for a moment today where you're given the choice to let something negative slip in. Recognize it. Refute it. And replace it with God's love.

Dear Lord, make me aware of where I'm off course. Give me the desire to do what pleases You. In Jesus' name, Amen.

REMEMBER

The decisions we make every second of every day matter. So, we fall hard upon soft grace, asking God to make us more sensitive, more aware, and more in tune with our constant need for forgiveness.

REFLECT

What small decisions have you made in the past that had major ramifications on your present? Think back to that moment when something small crept into your heart and pulled your focus from right to wrong.

RESPOND

Ask God to forgive you for that moment you reflected on. Now, picture yourself having to make a similar choice in the future. Decide now to choose the right way, and practice in your mind doing so.

POWER VERSES

James 3:16; Proverbs 27:4

When Life Breaks You

Samantha Evilsizer

... to bestow on them a crown
of beauty instead of ashes ...
(ISAIAH 61:3)

It was a hard year. Heartbreakin' hard.

Everything seemed to go up in flames. My heart was burned and the ashes seemed a safe place to fall—and to stay. Unresponsive to encouragement, I sat in ashes a *long* time. My hands filled with fists of ashes.

I needed to get up; I just couldn't muster the oomph to do it. Sadness felt natural; sorrow was comfortable. I knew I couldn't wallow in ashes forever. And here's the sweet thing: God knew this too. He unwaveringly knelt down next to me and extended a helping hand up. He promised: *Give Me the ashes; I'll do something with them. Something beautiful.*

He spoke this message in hundreds of ways, but it wasn't until I was at a concert that I understood the message He was giving me. It was barely noticeable. Permanently tattooed on the foot of the young woman sitting in front of me was God's message in a swirly font and dark ink: *Beauty for ashes.* And there He was. Our God of redemption and resurrection, speaking His timeless message once again—for me, for you. *Give Me the ashes; I'll do something with them. Something beautiful.*

It's now been several years since that concert. I wish I could tie up my story with a pretty bow. Say that I unclenched my fists, gave God the soot, and have been happy-go-lucky ever since. But I won't—because that's not the truth.

I want to be real. And real is that it took a long time to see anything redemptive in my heartbreak. Real is also my trust—my faith—in a God who makes life worth living. Even when I can't wrap my mind around life's crazy questions, I'll stay committed to taking Him at His Word, regardless of my circumstances; believing He is a loving Creator who is making beauty in my life even from ashes; hoping for what remains unseen.

I'll continue to look for His goodness because, truly, the most beautiful thing in the midst of pain is a faithful God. One who stands by. One who redeems—all things. One who creates masterpieces out of muck. A God who took the most hopeless situation and the ultimate death and resurrected hope. Resurrected our hope: Jesus.

Dear Lord, You are my Creator and I know You can work masterpieces out of muck. Today, I recommit myself in hope and faith to You. I'm looking up to You. Thank You for kneeling beside me, ever ready to give a helping hand. In Jesus' name, Amen.

REMEMBER

Our God is a God of redemption and resurrection, speaking His timeless message once again: *Give Me the ashes; I'll do something with them. Something beautiful.*

REFLECT

Consider the ways God is showing you He is exchanging your ashes for beauty. Don't forget the small ways too.

RESPOND

Take note of God's redemption today in the extraordinary things we can often take for ordinary: a flower pushing up through the dirt, a baby growing in its mother's womb, the rain watering the hard ground. Thank God for these things and for the redemption He's working in your life, even now.

POWER VERSES

Psalm 42:6; Psalm 6:4

If God Loves Me, Why . . . ?

Renee Swope

"For I know the plans I have for you,"
declares the LORD,
"plans to prosper you and not to harm you,
plans to give you hope and a future."
(JEREMIAH 29:11)

Soon after I surrendered my life to Christ, I started struggling with painful things from my past that made me doubt God's promises for my future. I wondered: *If God loves me, why has He allowed so much pain in my life?* Why had He allowed my family to be broken by adultery and divorce as well as alcohol and drug addictions? And why didn't He stop me from the pain I brought on myself?

One afternoon I told a friend about my doubts and questions. She didn't give me a pat answer; instead, she shared her own story of deep disappointments and brokenness. Yet, I didn't sense doubt or pain in her words, just a strong confidence and hope.

Turning the pages of her Bible to Jeremiah 29, Wanda read God's promise to me: "'For I know the plans I have for you,' declares the LORD 'plans to prosper you and not to harm you, plans to give you hope and a future.'"

She said God wanted to heal the pain of my past and use what I'd experienced to shape His plans for my future. But I didn't want God to use my pain or my past. I just wanted it to go away.

Have you ever wondered, *If God loves me, why . . . ?*

This is the kind of question that lingers in a heart that's been wounded and disappointed. And hurts that aren't healed can lead to bitterness and bondage. Yet, in the security of a relationship with Jesus, God invites us to ask hard questions and look for answers that usher us into the depths of His redeeming love and healing power.

May I whisper some hope into your heart today? *If you are living and breathing, your purpose has not yet been fulfilled. No matter what you have done or what has been done to you, God has a plan for your life.*

So, how do we discover God's plans? Let's read the premise that follows God's promise. After God declares the plans He has for us, He says: "Then you will call on me and come and pray to me, and I will listen to you. You will seek me and find me when you seek me with all your heart" (Jeremiah 29:12–13).

We find God's plans when we surrender ours to Him. It's a moment-by-moment process of coming to Him, talking to Him, and letting Him love us into a place of hope and healing.

God's love has the power to redeem and restore us into confident hope. When we allow the Holy Spirit, poured out like living water, to go deep into our pain, He can heal our hearts from the inside out. His truth cuts to the core of our struggles, bringing purpose to our pain, redemption from our past, and hope for our future!

Dear Lord, heal my hurts and give me hope as I learn to trust the plans You have for me. I'm seeking You with all my heart today. Set me free from my doubts and lead me into a place of confident hope. In Jesus' name, Amen.

REMEMBER

If you are living and breathing, your purpose has not yet been fulfilled. No matter what you have done or what has been done to you, God has a plan for your life.

REFLECT

What excites you about finding God's plans for your life?

RESPOND

Write out one dream you have for your life. Then ask the Lord if this dream is in line with His dream for you.

POWER VERSES

Psalm 71:5; Jeremiah 17:7

"Harmless" Little Lies?

Glynnis Whitwer

*"Whoever can be trusted with very little
can also be trusted with much,
and whoever is dishonest with very little
will also be dishonest with much."*

(LUKE 16:10)

My job was overwhelming, yet I was desperate to appear competent. As a young college graduate, I was grateful for the position. But over time, both the company and my work level grew to the point where I was drowning. And, as I fell farther behind, I began to give misleading responses to my boss.

My employer was very hands-on and often called me into her office for an update on my projects. I dreaded those meetings, knowing she'd be displeased with my lack of progress. And that is when the lies started: "Yes, that project is coming along nicely." "I'm almost finished." "Just waiting for a few more pieces of information."

After our meetings, I'd rush back to my desk and frantically try to make my progress match the inaccurate response I'd just given. Over time, the lies and truth became jumbled. I'd crossed a line of personal integrity that nagged at the edges of my conscience, but not enough to make a change. Until one day my boss gave me another request: to lie for her.

She hadn't gotten something done, and asked me to lie to someone else. This wasn't right. She hadn't even started the project. And now I was supposed to cover for her? It was as if God made me do a 180 and stare at the line of integrity I had already crossed.

I'd compromised my character one half-truth, one excuse, one rationalization at a time. But no more. I had some decisions to make. Would integrity be a mask I put on at church and took off at work? Was my career more important than my character?

Those were heavy questions for a young woman. But they were necessary. God used this situation to help shape the person He wanted me to be.

Knowing I could lose my job, with humility and respect I told my boss

I couldn't, no I wouldn't, lie for her. Amazingly, she didn't fire me. With a huff and a sigh, she accepted my decision.

While I wasn't up to confessing all my lies to her, I did confess them to God. And I made a commitment that day to honesty, no matter how personally difficult it was.

God cares about what may seem like harmless little lies: "Whoever can be trusted with very little can also be trusted with much, and whoever is dishonest with very little will also be dishonest with much" (Luke 16:10).

God was watching me then, and He's watching me now. Which is why every word I speak is important. Choosing truth is hard, especially when it reveals a weakness. Yet with God's help, I'm making progress to become the woman of integrity He's called me to be.

Dear Lord, You are the source of all truth. Forgive me for the times I've been deceptive in order to manipulate the opinions of others. I want to be a woman who is filled with Your truth. Help me to uncover whatever stands in the way of becoming that woman. In Jesus' name, Amen.

REMEMBER

Choosing to live without a shadow of dishonesty will establish you as a trustworthy woman before God and others.

REFLECT

Is there an area of your life where you are less than 100 percent honest? If so, confess that to God in prayer. What little decisions of integrity can you make to help strengthen your character?

RESPOND

Keep a pad of paper and pen with you today and make a tick mark every time you are not 100 percent honest. Confess these instances to the Lord at the end of the day, and ask Him to help you use this exercise as a reminder to always strive to speak the truth (in love).

POWER VERSES

2 Corinthians 8:21; 1 Peter 2:12

Calming the Mama Drama

Lynn Cowell

Be completely humble and gentle;
be patient, bearing with one another in love.
(EPHESIANS 4:2)

Oversleeping on school picture day is not a great way to start the morning. I ran to my daughters' rooms, blurting out words of panic. At first they groaned, "Oh no! Not today!"

I braced myself, sure that the drama would start at any moment. Yet minutes later, I heard silliness and singing. I heard kindness instead of quarreling. They chose *not* to take out the stress on each other.

I wish I could say my girls learned this from me, but that's not the case. In fact, God has been working on me about my own mama drama, challenging me with truths that instruct me to be "completely humble and gentle ... patient, bearing with one another in love."

Too often, when my expectations aren't met or I'm faced with things I can't control, my emotions spin out of control. Before I know it, I'm talking before I even think about what I'm saying. All that wise instruction about being humble, gentle, and patient is quickly forgotten.

What about you? Do you ever yell at your kids or let frustrations mount when things don't go as planned? Do you suffer from a little mama drama?

That morning God gave me another opportunity to choose humility, gentleness, and patience with my girls. As we were walking out the door, I realized I had not filled out the picture order forms. Scrambling to find the papers and my checkbook, I felt the pressure mounting again.

I had a choice: let my emotions explode or choose humility.

Thankfully, I paused and gave way to the Holy Spirit's leading. And my desire for peace to become my new norm and to leave mama drama behind was successful!

So, how do we choose humility and patience when dealing with our kids?

If time allows, I've found it helpful to pull away from the situation and give myself a time-out. Removing myself affords me the opportunity to ask God to help me regroup my runaway emotions and submit my thoughts to the control of the Holy Spirit. Pulling away also shows my kids the benefits—patience and gentleness, for example—that result when I don't allow my emotions to rule over me. If there isn't time to physically remove myself, there is always enough time to take a deep breath and invite the Holy Spirit to bring me wisdom and self-control.

When we surrender our emotions, actions, and reactions to God, peace can become our new norm as we leave mama drama behind!

Dear Lord, help me to leave behind mama drama and use me to be a peacemaker in my home. I want to learn to give myself a time-out and ask the Holy Spirit to enter each stressful situation in which I find myself. In Jesus' name, Amen.

REMEMBER

When you surrender your emotions, actions, and reactions to God, peace can become your new norm.

REFLECT

When does God have to exercise His gentleness and patience toward you? How might He help you, in turn, display that same gentleness and patience toward others in your life?

RESPOND

Spy on your life today, looking for opportunities to exercise humility, gentleness, and patience. Ask the Holy Spirit to help you see these opportunities and give you the power to respond.

POWER VERSES

James 1:5; 1 Timothy 6:11

A Complete Waste of Time

Lysa TerKeurst

Do not be quickly provoked in your spirit,
for anger resides in the lap of fools.
(ECCLESIASTES 7:9)

My daughter Brooke got in the car the other day and sighed. It was one of those sighs that said, *I'm going through something, but unless you ask me, I'm not freely revealing this information.*

I casually inquired, "Tell me the high from your day and then tell me your low."

"Mom," she groaned, letting me know she secretly loved that I was asking, but all the middle school in her was making her play it cool.

I waited quietly, knowing she would eventually tell me. And she did. Something hard had happened at school that day.

I put my hand on hers. "I'm so sorry, sweetheart. I know that makes you sad."

To my surprise, this normally emotional child said, "Actually, no. I've decided sometimes being sad or mad over stuff like this is a complete waste of my time."

And just like that she smiled and was ready to get on with the rest of her day. No tears. No tirade. No lamenting and wearing herself out with a tidal wave of emotion while overprocessing this hard situation. Simply a thirteen-year-old's decision that sometimes it's just not worth all that. The child-turned-tutor. The young one doling out wisdom.

Sometimes being sad or mad over stuff like this is a complete waste of my time.

I've mulled over her statement a hundred times. It's good. It's truth. Indeed, there are things to be sad about, but so much of what pulls at my emotions isn't worth the time and energy I give it.

I love how Ecclesiastes 7:9 reads in *The Message*: "Don't be quick to fly off the handle. Anger boomerangs. You can spot a fool by the lumps on his head." Oh how I don't want to be that fool! Hurt feelings are hard enough; but they're made so much worse when we react negatively to them. We just end up hurting ourselves worse.

Is there something you've been sad or mad about that maybe is a waste of your time? Ask God to help you have a different perspective today.

Dear Lord, some days my emotions seem to steamroll right over me. Please help me reconnect with You and know that many times being sad or mad over stuff is a complete waste of my time. I'd rather focus on You. In Jesus' name, Amen.

REMEMBER

Sometimes being sad or mad over stuff is a complete waste of time.

REFLECT

How does reacting negatively to hurt feelings help in healing? How does it hinder? Recognize the difference in the two reactions.

RESPOND

Replace a moment of anger or sadness with praises to the Lord today.

POWER VERSES

James 1:19–21; Proverbs 14:29

Living in a Season of "How Long?"

Wendy Pope

How long, LORD? Will you forget me forever?
How long will you hide your face from me?
(PSALM 13:1)

Several years ago, my husband, Scott, began to experience extreme and unexpected health problems. We had no idea when or if he'd get better. Weeks and months dragged by. Constantly wondering, *How long?* took its toll on us. The unrelenting stress of an uncertain future weakened my faith and I began to wonder if God had forgotten me. I felt tired, lonely, and despairing. I wanted out.

King David was once in a similar place of questioning God: "How long, LORD? Will you forget me forever? How long will you hide your face from me?" (Psalm 13:1). David's circumstances had turned from promising to life threatening.

He'd been anointed king but didn't step into his role immediately. While he waited for God's plan to come to fruition, he served the current king, Saul. David gained respect and affection from the people of Israel, as well as those in King Saul's court. Because of this, Saul became jealous of David and frequently threatened his life.

David wrote Psalm 13 when he was on the run from King Saul and found himself in a hard place of losing hope. He needed encouragement and strength. From a place of darkness and desperation, he cried out to God, "How long?"

Are you living in the unbearable days of "how long?" *How long will I be unemployed? How long will my child be a prodigal? How long will I live with this life-threatening diagnosis? How long will I be lonely?*

God used David's words to strengthen Scott's faith and mine. Praying his words in Psalm 13 renewed our communication with God by helping us realize the "right" words weren't necessary. We could simply let the words filling our hearts fall from our lips as we cried out to God for help. Our strengthened faith equipped us to walk the long medical road to a diagnosis, treatment plan, and trust in God's faithfulness through our "how long?"

> *Dear Lord, thank You for King David's vulnerability. His words strengthen my faith and renew my hope for deliverance from my "how long?" Thank You for allowing me to pour out my heart to You when I am discouraged and need help and hope. In Jesus' name, Amen.*

REMEMBER

God uses every "how long?" to strengthen my faith and show me His power.

REFLECT

What spiritual benefits are fashioned as we live in "how long?"

RESPOND

If you are currently living in a difficult season, take some quiet time out of your day to write your own "how long?" psalm. Let the words that fill your heart pour out onto the page.

POWER VERSES

Psalm 17:1; Psalm 51:15

Do I Really "Get" God?

Micca Campbell

He who forms the mountains, who creates the wind,
and who reveals his thoughts to mankind,
who turns dawn to darkness,
and treads on the heights of the earth—
the LORD God Almighty is his name.

(AMOS 4:13)

Doing laundry. Raising well-adjusted kids. Building a good relationship with my husband. Even answering the phone. So often I feel like the responsibility for everything in my life depends on me. And honestly, I doubt my ability to get it all done, and do it all well.

I know I'm not alone in feeling this way. Who doesn't feel the pressure of higher grocery bills and mouths to feed? What employee doesn't carry the weight of doing a good job? What mother doesn't fear her child will give in to peer pressure? These concerns and a thousand others tangle our thoughts into anxious knots. When we feel as if everything depends on us, we carry a heavy burden.

But we're not alone or solely responsible for making things turn out fine. When I feel alone, I've forgotten God is always with me. And when I feel incapable, it's usually because I've forgotten to acknowledge God's presence and power. However, looking to God's presence and power won't help us if we don't believe He is truly sovereign. We need to know and believe just how mighty God is. Otherwise, we'll look at our limitations and feel like they limit Him. We'll end up with a God who is only a little bigger, a little stronger, and a little wiser than us. That makes God small. And when we have a small God, we feel like He depends on us to do a good job ... just like everyone else does.

I felt this way when I became a parent. I thought if I read all the how-to books, I could do a good job. I believed the lie that happy, successful children depended on my efforts. Which made me feel very stressed and alone. It wasn't until I started to "get" God and grasp the wisdom and guidance He provides that I learned to depend on His provision and direction. I no longer felt like I had to raise my kids based solely on my own knowledge and efforts.

God never intended for us to live under the pressure of everything depending on us. It's when we lean on Him instead of ourselves that we experience supernatural strength and provision. Reflect on the wisdom of Amos 4:13 and meditate on God's greatness. If the Lord can do all this, surely He can equip us for whatever our daily tasks may be—from parenting challenges to project deadlines to folding mountains of laundry.

On the other hand, if we set out to make ourselves the measure of all things, we will never experience the full benefit of God's greatness. It doesn't have to be this way. Having the right understanding of God frees us from the weight of carrying our burdens alone and allows us to rest in His exceptional power and presence.

Dear Lord, set my sights on You and Your great attributes. Help me to live in Your presence, dependent on Your guidance each day. In Jesus' name, Amen.

REMEMBER

God is bigger, stronger, and wiser than you are. You do not have to carry your burdens alone.

REFLECT

In what ways have you envisioned God to be nothing more than a super-sized version of yourself? How can reflecting on His true attributes infuse you with strength?

RESPOND

Whenever you feel frustrated, weak, and alone this week, reassure yourself of God's promised presence. Apply these truths—"I can't, God can" and "I'm going to let Him"—to every situation you face.

POWER VERSES

Ephesians 3:16; 2 Corinthians 12:9

But I Have a Right to Be Angry

Tracie Miles

Understand this, my dear brothers and sisters:
You must all be quick to listen, slow to speak, and slow to get angry.
Human anger does not produce the righteousness God desires.
(JAMES 1:19–20 NLT)

I had been lied to, betrayed, and hurt. I was angry and felt I had every right to be. Anger crushed my desire to forgive. Although I'd asked God to fill my heart with mercy, I kept a running mental list of justifications for my anger that overrode my empty prayers.

My internal dialogue was one big argument. One voice tried to convince me I was justified in remaining angry; another voice tried to persuade me that mercy was the right choice. For months, the loudest voice was the one that indulged my damaged emotions: *Yes, I have a right to be angry. Anyone would agree.*

Listening to the voice of bitterness and unforgiveness, I often lashed out with impatience and meanness. I could play the good Christian girl for short periods of time, but if something triggered my suppressed emotions, hostility and resentment catapulted to the surface.

Reading Scripture one morning, I sensed God inviting me to consider the direction my anger was taking me and the damage it was doing. As I read the words from James 1, I couldn't help but notice how it says "everyone" should be slow to speak and slow to anger. This truth from God's Word left no room for my excuses or righteous indignation, even though I felt like my anger was justified. And then a few verses later, I read this: "Do not merely listen to the word, and so deceive yourselves. Do what it says" (James 1:22).

From a worldly perspective, I knew I had every right to be angry. But from God's perspective, my anger only added to the sin of the situation. My refusal to extend the same mercy and forgiveness God had given me was preventing me from living out the gospel.

Through the words of James, God softened my heart. I acknowledged that although I said I'd forgiven this person with my words, I had not forgiven with my heart—and it was time to do so and move on.

In every area of life, including managing our most powerful emotions, God tells us to be quick to listen (to Him and others), slow to speak, and slow to become angry. As we apply these practices in our relationships, we become doers of His Word, not just hearers, and that leads to the righteousness God desires.

Dear Lord, please forgive me for harboring anger. Equip me with a supernatural ability to forgive those who have hurt me. Guard my heart when old emotions threaten to surface. Strip my heart of anger and replace it with joy. In Jesus' name, Amen.

REMEMBER

Anger only worsens any situation, but selfless forgiveness brings freedom. We are all called to forgive even when wronged, just as God forgives us.

REFLECT

Whom have you been harboring anger toward or withholding forgiveness from? Have these feelings caused you to feel bitter?

RESPOND

Pour out your heart to God today, telling Him how you feel. Then write out a prayer of forgiveness for the one who hurt you, surrendering that burden to God, and asking Him to replace your feelings of bitterness with peace and joy.

POWER VERSES

Ephesians 4:26–27; Ephesians 4:30–31

On Eagles' Wings

T. Suzanne Eller

But those who trust in the LORD will find new strength.
They will soar high on wings like eagles.
They will run and not grow weary.
They will walk and not faint.
(ISAIAH 40:31 NLT)

My children ran up the steep path, unaware Mom was left behind. Their shouts of "I'll beat you to the top!" filtered down. I sat on the large rock, my head on my arms, tears running down my face.

The park was our favorite place to picnic and explore. My children and I hadn't visited in a long time because chemotherapy, radiation, and two surgeries had overtaken my calendar. With my treatments finally ended, I wanted nothing more than to return to normal life again. But I was exhausted. Things that once came easily now seemed impossible. Like climbing the steep, rocky path to the top of the hill. I used to run up these rocks, laughing with my children. Now I could only walk partway up. My stamina dipped below zero.

As I sat there, I wondered: *Will life ever be the same? Will I ever be the same?*

It's now been two decades since I sat on the rock and cried. It hardly seems possible! My young children are grown and I'm a grandma to four beautiful babies. Advanced-stage breast cancer robbed me of much—certainty about my future, the security of my children, and for a time, my health. But it didn't rob me of my faith. When I remember that moment on the rock, I don't see a young mom sitting alone; I see a woman whom God is holding tight.

There are times when our strength isn't enough, when our wings feel heavy. In those times God invites us to rely on Him. God's promise through the prophet Isaiah is that when we are weary, we can soar like eagles. It's not our strength that causes us to soar, but God's strength as He lifts us up and out of our weary places—in *His* might.

It took months before I recovered fully and could once again run up the trail with my children. But the path I learned to follow closely during that time was into the pages of His Word, where encouragement filled this embattled mom with hope. After two surgeries, chemotherapy, and radiation, I wasn't physically strong enough to do anything on my own, but I found spiritual strength in God's promises. I depended on God to give me energy when I felt weak. And I celebrated the smallest of victories even when they didn't seem like much.

Are you exhausted today? You aren't alone. You can trust Him to lift your wings, to give you new strength and power, as you depend on Him each moment.

Dear Father, I'm tired and I cannot do this on my own. Today, I take my eyes off of what I cannot do and I place my focus on You—on Your promises, on Your Word. Lift my wings with Your strength and help me fly again. In Jesus' name, Amen.

REMEMBER

You were never intended to fight life's battles alone. It's not your strength that causes you to soar, but God lifts you up and out of your weary places —in *His* might.

REFLECT

How will you celebrate your smallest victory today in a big way?

RESPOND

Invite God into your challenge, but with a twist. Choose a day to celebrate. Share God's faithfulness with a friend who is facing similar challenges.

POWER VERSES

Psalm 103:1, 5; Exodus 19:4

Chasing Love

Lysa TerKeurst

I spread out my hands to you;
I thirst for you like a parched land.

(PSALM 143:6)

Tears streamed down her beautiful face as we talked. Just six months ago, her world had been filled with love — a devoted husband, a healthy toddler, fun friends. Life was full.

But some part of her heart still felt a little empty. She couldn't put her finger on it. She tried talking to friends, but they laughed it off as hormones that would pass. Only the feeling didn't pass. She felt detached from her husband and disappointed that his love didn't fulfill her. She'd always thought of marriage as the ultimate love. He was going to be the one to right her wrongs and fill her insecurities, or so she thought.

Questions bombarded her. *What's wrong with him? Why doesn't he say what he's supposed to say? Maybe it's me. Maybe I'm not pretty enough, witty enough, good enough.*

Then she met a man who said things she'd longed to hear her husband say. He made her feel pretty and witty. She rationalized that she'd never really loved her husband and that this new man was her true soul mate. She fell into his arms and spun a web of lies. The thrill of new romance clouded every decision.

She had not wanted to come to the women's retreat. She knew it might make her feel guilty and she was well beyond guilty feelings. She was just waiting for the right time to leave her husband and start over with the real love of her life. But her friends had started to grow suspicious about her reluctance to attend. To appease them, she went.

Over the course of the retreat, the walls she'd carefully constructed to keep everyone at a distance crumbled. She confessed it all. When she approached me after one of the sessions, she desperately wanted to know how I felt so full of God's love. She'd never known that kind of relationship with God. She was now convinced it wasn't the love of another man her heart craved; it was the love of God.

This is true for many people. We spend years chasing things we think will make us feel loved. But everything this world offers is temporary. The kind of love our souls crave is eternal. And only God can fill us with that kind of love.

Chasing love outside the will of God invites the exact opposite of love. Here is a picture of God's perfect love: It is patient, kind ... doesn't envy ... it's not self-seeking ... does not delight in evil but rejoices with the truth ... it always protects ... always perseveres. Love never fails (1 Corinthians 13:4–8).

This isn't a description of what is ours when we fall in love with another person. It is a description of God's love. The kind of love our souls crave will never be found in the things of this world. Lasting and perfectly satisfying love will only be found when we stop chasing other people and things and start living out the truths of God.

Dear Lord, please help me see marriage for the sacred gift that it is. And help me to be ultimately satisfied in Your love. In Jesus' name, Amen.

REMEMBER

The kind of love your soul craves is eternal. And only God can fill you with that kind of love.

REFLECT

How does it make you feel to consider allowing God to fill your deepest needs? What would change if you gave Him room to love you?

RESPOND

Make plans to take a weekend retreat to reconnect with the Lord. Check with your church to see if they have one coming up, or arrange to do one with a few close girlfriends.

POWER VERSES

Ephesians 1:4; Matthew 19:26

A Sparkling Confession

Rachel Olsen

The integrity of the upright guides them,
but the unfaithful are destroyed by their duplicity.
(PROVERBS 11:3)

I secretly picked up the ring from the display and slipped it onto my young finger. I then clasped my hands behind my back as my mom and I exited the store.

Once in the car, I admired my new ring.

On some level, I knew it was wrong because I hadn't asked Mom if I could have it. But the store I had taken it from was owned by my parents. *Didn't that also make it mine?* Apparently, age five is not too young to rationalize.

It's also not too young to learn about integrity. I've often heard it said that integrity is what you do when no one is watching. When no one was watching, I stole a ring.

My mom noticed my preoccupation with the ring and asked where I'd gotten it. I told her a friend had given it to me. She knew better. She told me that if I refused to tell the truth she, and others, wouldn't be able to trust me. And she told me that if I didn't confess and correct my mistakes when I realized them, I'd feel awful with guilt. She gently warned me that ignoring that guilt would eventually harden my heart.

I asked my mom to turn the car around; I needed to go back to the store. She didn't let me quietly put the ring back. She instructed me to tell the lady working the register what I'd done, and to apologize.

I was torn. Part of me wanted to come clean. But part of me didn't want this lady to think less of me for stealing. I loved visiting our store—all the employees treated me so well. I feared confessing would cost me their favor.

Billy Graham once said:

Integrity is the glue that holds our way of life together. We must constantly strive to keep our integrity intact. When wealth is lost, nothing is lost. When health is lost, something is lost. When character is lost, all is lost.

The Bible says it this way: "The integrity of the upright guides them, but the unfaithful are destroyed by their duplicity" (Proverbs 11:3).

I nervously set the ring on the counter and told the clerk I'd taken it. She furrowed her brow and told me that was wrong, and instructed me never to do it again. Then she smiled, picked me up, and told me that stolen things lose their sparkle, but that an honest girl never would. My five-year-old heart wanted to be the kind of girl that sparkles. (And my grown-up heart hasn't changed much.)

If your heart wants you to be the kind of woman who sparkles, decide today to do the right thing. Tell the truth. Flee from temptation. Ask forgiveness. Although it may be hard—it may even seem costly—integrity will guide us safely. Jesus said it also enables us to see God (Matthew 5:8). And it will ultimately help us to shine with integrity.

Dear Lord, I want my life to be bright with integrity. I want a pure heart that pleases You. Forgive my sins and help me walk in a manner worthy of You. In Jesus' name, Amen.

REMEMBER

Integrity is like glue that holds our way of life and our relationships together.

REFLECT

For what recent wrong do you need to confess, apologize, or make amends?

RESPOND

Journal your confession and your decision about how to respond to the person you've wronged. Make amends where you can today.

POWER VERSES

Proverbs 20:7, 11; Proverbs 12:22

When You Feel Like You're Not Enough

Renee Swope

When Jesus spoke again to the people, he said,
"I am the light of the world.
Whoever follows me will never walk in darkness,
but will have the light of life."

(JOHN 8:12)

I had that awful feeling of not being *enough* ... not smart enough, not good enough. For weeks, I felt inadequate in every way—from the way I parented, to the way I served God in ministry, to the way I organized my time.

One afternoon as I was putting on makeup, I noticed how the bathroom light threw a huge shadow on the wall behind me. As I stood there looking at the shadow, it dawned on me: *All of my insecurities were creating a huge shadow over my soul—a shadow of doubt.*

That day, I came to two important realizations. First, I was the one creating the shadow by blocking the light. And second, I could only see the shadow when I turned away from the light.

Shadows are created all around us when something blocks light, and so it is with the shadow of doubt. When we focus our thoughts on ourselves—how inadequate we feel, or what others think about us, or how we're performing—we cast a shadow of doubt by blocking the light of God's truth. But we were not designed to block the light. We were created to live in the light by focusing on what God thinks about us instead of what we think about ourselves.

Jesus said, "I am the light of the world. Whoever follows me will never walk in darkness, but will have the light of life" (John 8:12). When we follow Jesus closely and focus our thoughts on Him, we can live beyond the shadow of our doubts and find lasting confidence in Him.

That afternoon, I realized I had to purposefully shift my focus from my feelings of inadequacy to God's promises of His sufficiency and grace in my life. I had to choose to focus on truth (the light of Christ) so I could exchange my feelings of low self-confidence for lasting soul-confidence.

The next time you feel your heart dwelling in the shadow of self-doubt, ask God to help you turn toward the light of Christ as you focus your thoughts on His truths about you.

When you feel inadequate, God says, *You are chosen*: "'You are my witnesses,' declares the LORD, 'and my servant whom I have chosen, so that you may know and believe me and understand that I am he'" (Isaiah 43:10).

When you feel unstable, God says, *You are able*: "The Sovereign LORD is my strength; he makes my feet like the feet of a deer, he enables me to tread on the heights" (Habakkuk 3:19).

When you feel unworthy, God says, *You are precious and loved*: "You are precious and honored in my sight, and … I love you" (Isaiah 43:4).

Dear Lord, help me to live beyond the shadows of my doubts as I follow and focus on the light of Your truth today. In Jesus' name, Amen.

REMEMBER

When you feel inadequate, God says, "You are chosen." When you feel unstable, God says, "You are able." When you feel unworthy, God says, "You are precious and loved."

REFLECT

What are your most common thoughts of self-doubt? How do they make you feel? Inadequate? Uncertain? Indecisive?

RESPOND

Write your self-doubts in pencil on a white piece of paper. Then write, "I am chosen, I am able, I am precious and loved," in dark marker over them. Hold the paper up to the light and see how the bold words overshadow the penciled words. Let this serve as a visual reminder of how God's truths overshadow your self-doubts.

POWER VERSES

Romans 8:6; John 1:4

What My Checkbook Says about Me

Glynnis Whitwer

One person gives freely, yet gains even more;
another withholds unduly, but comes to poverty.

(PROVERBS 11:24)

Imagine walking into church one day to discover all your financial information on display. Your check register is included as a bulletin insert. Your bank statement is in the pastor's PowerPoint presentation and the message that day is based on how you spent your money last week. How would you respond? Would you sprint out the back door, horrified at the thought of your spending habits being exposed? Or would you perhaps feel a little uncomfortable but trust that your spending was in sync with your values?

The way we handle money—how we earn it, spend it, and give it away—shows what's important to us. A peek inside our checkbooks reveals what we value most.

In the early years of our marriage, our checkbook definitely revealed the truth about what I valued and trusted—and it wasn't God. My husband wanted to give 10 percent of our income to the church, and I continually talked him out of it, bargaining the percentage down with the promise of increasing it over time. My lack of faith (in God and my husband) shouted through the entries in my check register.

Years later, I finally gave in to my husband's repeated requests to tithe. Sadly, it wasn't with serene faith and confidence. Rather, I secretly believed I'd be able to say, "I told you so" once and for all. Imagine my surprise when God proved Himself faithful in spite of my unfaithfulness.

I learned a life-changing lesson: God can be trusted. Listening to great sermons didn't teach me this. Hearing how God answered my friend's prayer didn't teach me this. I had to learn it for myself. In doing so, I learned that one of the best ways to experience God's trustworthiness is in the area of finances.

Though many of us are uncomfortable talking about money, the Bible refers to it more than two thousand times. God knows that how we manage this part of life is important to being an effective Christian, particularly because few people will ever see the details of our obedience in this area.

Holding money with an open hand shows we trust God. He's given us everything we have: our health, our jobs, our homes, and our financial resources. Giving back to God shows we trust that His Word is true and that we trust Him to provide for our needs.

At the heart of the decision to give money to God is whether or not He can be trusted. The answer is yes — God can be trusted! Today, through the grace of God, my checkbook lines up with my values and my profession of faith.

Dear Lord, You are worthy of all my trust. Forgive the times I doubt You and choose to trust myself. Thank You for giving me another chance to obey Your command to give with a generous heart. Help me to be a woman who lives out her faith in her checkbook as well as her words. In Jesus' name, Amen.

REMEMBER

How we handle money reveals what we really value most in life.

REFLECT

Take a look at your bank statement or check register for the past few months. What do your spending habits (as well as what you *don't* spend money on) reveal about your values?

RESPOND

Commit to keep a spending diary for one week. As you enter expenses, take time to pray, asking God if there's anything He wants you to change.

POWER VERSES

Deuteronomy 14:23; Malachi 3:10

When People Drive You Crazy

Luann Prater

If it is possible, as far as it depends on you,
live at peace with everyone.
(ROMANS 12:18)

The apostle Paul's challenge in Romans 12 is to do everything we can to live at peace with everyone. Easier said than done, right?

One way God helps me do this is by regularly placing what I call "grinders" in my life. Grinders are people who grind me until all my shine is worn away. They drive me crazy!

Not long ago, I met a woman I'll call Sue, who decided she must become my best friend. We didn't have much in common, but that didn't stop Sue from calling, texting, and emailing—first occasionally, then constantly. She thought I could fill a hole in her life. Unfortunately, her behavior began to wear a hole in mine.

When I didn't have time to talk or respond, she became agitated and hurt. It was obvious this friendship was capsizing and in need of a checkup. When a relationship like this begins to wear me out, absorb my life, or create chaos, I ask myself three questions.

Have I listened with compassion and responded in love? It's important to evaluate my behavior to see if I'm contributing to the toxicity in the relationship. Every situation has many factors and owning my part is key.

What limits do I need to set? I decide what's healthy for me and draw a line there. How much time can I reasonably give? What am I willing to sacrifice to invest in this relationship? I pray that God will help me to establish and maintain those boundaries and then I discuss and define them with my grinder.

Is it time to walk away? Paul uses an important phrase, "If it is possible . . ." That means there may be times when it's *not* possible. I may need to part ways with someone for a season. God can redeem anything and often He brings folks back together after a time of separation.

As for Sue, I asked myself if I'd listened with compassion and responded in love. I prayed for God to highlight my behavior and point out any flaws in my reactions. He showed me some boundaries I needed to set with Sue in order to live at peace with her.

I took her to lunch and apologized for not being clear with my limits and time constraints. We prayed together and asked God to fill the empty places in both of our lives. She appreciated the honesty and promised to honor our newly set boundary lines. Instead of sinking, our friendship became a sweet treasure.

Confronting difficult people is hard, but important. We do it to limit the negative impact they have on us and to live at peace with them. Our first step is putting our focus on the Prince of Peace and then on our own behavior.

Dear Lord, it's easy to fall into relationships that grind away my strength. Refocus my attention on You and show me how You want me to respond. Teach me how to set healthy boundaries in all of my relationships. May I always reflect Your Son. In Jesus' name, Amen.

REMEMBER

Sometimes you need to set boundaries in order to live at peace with others.

REFLECT

Have you listened with compassion and responded in love? What limits do you need to set? Is it time to walk away?

RESPOND

Write down a list of any grinders in your life right now. Walk through the three steps above for one of those people and then pray for him or her.

POWER VERSES

Romans 14:19; Proverbs 16:7

Bad Moments Don't Make Bad Moms

Lysa TerKeurst

But because of his great love for us, God,
who is rich in mercy, made us alive with Christ
even when we were dead in transgressions—
it is by grace you have been saved.

(EPHESIANS 2:4–5)

Do you ever feel like the ping-pong ball in a heated match between your good mom self and your bad mom self? Here is how this vicious game works in my life ...

Much to my daughter's delight, I volunteer to keep the class guinea pig over spring break. *Good mom!*

Two weeks before spring break, our pet hamster has an accident and makes an early exit from this world. I get a letter from the principal informing me that, due to the unfortunate hamster situation, we have been deemed unfit guinea pig babysitters. *Bad mom!*

I delight the teacher by showing up on time to read to the class. *Good mom!*

That same day, I get an email from a teacher listing three parents who haven't turned in permission slips and I'm on the list for all the world to see. *Bad mom!*

I make sure my kids pack something healthy for lunch. *Good mom!*

The schedule falls apart and I feed them sugary cereal for dinner. *Bad mom!*

I desperately want to be a good mom. And sometimes I feel like I am—when life is clicking along with good attitudes, healthy hamsters, turned-in permission slips, and a pot roast for dinner. But let's be honest. The days where everything turns out right are sometimes few and far between. And I find myself feeling like a failure.

I need the truth of the apostle Paul's promise: "But because of his great love for us, God, who is rich in mercy, made us alive with Christ even when we were dead in transgressions—it is by grace you have been saved" (Ephesians 2:4–5). God's grace is always willing to step in. Not that it excuses me from being more patient, organized, or responsible, but it reminds me of what I need to hear: *Lysa, you are doing better than you think you are. My love for you is great! Stop bouncing from feeling good to bad to good to bad. In the good times, rejoice and thank Me. In the not so good times, call out to Me quickly.*

With God, we're never bad moms. We might be having a bad moment … or two … or seventeen. But a few bad moments do not define us. God's grace is there to cover us; teach us; and even in the middle of a bad moment, interrupt us, redirect us, and change us.

You are a good mom, my friend—even if, like me, you've had a few bad moments. You are the exact mom God knew these children needed. Live in that truth today.

Dear Lord, I'm thankful Your grace is always there to cover me.
Help me to stop bouncing between feeling good and feeling bad.
Teach me, redirect me, and change me today. In Jesus' name, Amen.

REMEMBER

You might be having a bad moment … or two … or seventeen. But God's grace is there to cover and teach you.

REFLECT

Think back on moments you've felt like a bad mom. What ways can you see God's grace in showing you were actually a good mom?

RESPOND

Set an example for your children today by finding the good in something they do for which you normally would scold them. For example, if they spill their milk while pouring it, instead of getting upset at the mess, praise them for their help in cleaning it up.

POWER VERSES

Colossians 3:15; Colossians 2:13

The Bitter Root

Wendy Blight

*See to it that no one falls short of the grace of God
and that no bitter root grows up to cause trouble and defile many.*
(HEBREWS 12:15)

How dare she ask this of me? I reread her email, which fueled my fury. Rather than reply immediately, I decided to forward the note to my husband for his advice. Any words I would've written to her directly would not have been kind.

Bitterness took root as I typed, and I spewed out my frustration. When I finished, I reviewed my message with great satisfaction. I'd expressed myself well to a safe person. Then I pressed SEND.

In that moment, I glanced at the TO box. I was horrified when I realized I'd hit REPLY instead of FORWARD. My heart sank. All my hurtful words and anger were now en route to her, not my husband.

I felt sick. *What should I do?* I picked up the phone and called my husband at work. We both agreed I needed to email her, explain what happened, and ask forgiveness. It was the hardest email I've ever written.

Her gracious response astounded me. She thanked me for my apology and closed her response with these words: "I forgive you, so let's just put this behind us." Her words of forgiveness melted the bitterness that had consumed my heart just an hour before. I'm sure she was hurt. My words were harsh. Yet she chose to overlook and pardon my offense.

It's easy to forget that we have choices when we're offended. We can surrender our hurt or hold on to our hurt. We can extend grace or harbor bitterness.

Bitterness is like poison that infects our lives. The author of Hebrews compares bitterness to a root that overtakes our hearts and causes trouble in many other areas of our lives (Hebrews 12:15). Although our feelings of bitterness, anger, and resentment may seem justified, they are not. Instead, they're hurtful and destructive—to ourselves as well as to the person who hurt us.

God's Word teaches us to forgive and instructs us not to let the sun go down while we're angry. When we do, we give the devil a place to work in our hearts and relationships. Instead of allowing the enemy room to plant relational weeds between us, my friend chose forgiveness, extended grace, and prevented a bitter root from taking hold.

She became a living example of the apostle Paul's words to the believers at Ephesus: "Be kind and compassionate to one another, forgiving each other, just as in Christ God forgave you" (Ephesians 4:32). Her wise example helped me move beyond my anger. My friend's gracious decision modeled humility. Her choice to forgive salvaged our friendship and changed how I react toward others who offend me. From that day forward, I've prayed that God's grace would flow through me, leaving no room for bitter roots.

Dear Lord, search my heart. See if there is any bitterness in me. Lead me to forgiveness. Enable me through the power of Your Holy Spirit to let go of all bitterness and to extend Your amazing grace. In Jesus' name, Amen.

REMEMBER

Choosing forgiveness is the only way to prevent a bitter root from taking hold in your heart and growing.

REFLECT

Is there someone against whom you harbor unforgiveness? What is it that keeps you from being able to forgive this person?

RESPOND

Review the verses shared in this devotion. Prayerfully ask God what your next step is with this person. Ask Him to equip you to take that first step, and then take it.

POWER VERSES

Colossians 3:13; Romans 12:9

The Trials of Friendship

Melissa Taylor

A friend loves at all times,
and a brother is born for a time of adversity.
(PROVERBS 17:17)

When I asked "Paula" if she could get together Thursday evening, she said she couldn't, but was obviously reluctant to give me a reason why. A little while later, I called "Dana" to see if she could hang out Thursday. You can imagine my surprise when she said, "Sorry, I'm going to a dinner party at Paula's."

Ouch! I wondered why Paula didn't just tell me about her dinner party. I felt left out and lied to. I struggled with whether or not I should approach Paula. I wanted to be able to say to her, "It's okay you didn't invite me, but I wish you had been truthful about why. I forgive you, because 'a friend loves at all times.'" But I was too afraid to even have the conversation.

At times like this, I follow my mom's advice: "When you don't know what to do, that's your cue to pray." So I prayed. God reminded me that being a friend who loves at all times means believing the best about each other and working through problems. However, despite what I knew from both my mom's wisdom and God's, I decided to just let it go. I was too fearful to confront my friend.

Paula called me a few weeks later. She too had been thinking about the party and felt bad for her lack of truthfulness to me. She apologized and explained why she hadn't invited me. I apologized for not confronting her. We ended up laughing about our insecurities; we knew we loved each other and wouldn't intentionally hurt one another. She could have been honest, and I could have been braver.

Dishonesty isn't supposed to be a part of friendship; neither is fear. Every relationship will have trials. But through them, we must believe the best about each other and forgive. When an obstacle comes between friends, it can eat at our hearts, little by little. When we allow it to build up over time, our enemy will use it to divide us.

Perhaps the Lord is prompting you to tell the truth to a friend with whom you've been dishonest. Or maybe you're the one has felt lied to. The wisdom of Scripture is this: "If it is possible, as far as it depends on you, live at peace with everyone" (Romans 12:18). Whether we are telling the truth or confronting a lie, reconciliation is a choice that is ours to make.

You may be on the end of a confession or confrontation that was not well received. It's painful to lose a friend. But rest assured, once we've done our part, the Lord will do His and heal the wound. If you're at a crossroads, wondering if you should confess or caringly confront, pray and take the next step. "A friend loves at all times" (Proverbs 17:17). Choosing to love at all times is not always easy, but in the end, it's worth it.

Dear Lord, I can make life more complicated than it needs to be.
Help me to be honest and brave, and to forgive others the way You
forgive me. In Jesus' name, Amen.

REMEMBER

While it isn't always easy to "love at all times," with God's help you can love and confront difficult issues in friendship.

REFLECT

Does one of your friendships need restoration or reconciliation? What fears or concerns do you have about the process? Pray about how to move into action to make things right.

RESPOND

Write a letter to a friend or relative with whom you need to reconcile. Put it in an envelope and pray about mailing it.

POWER VERSES

Matthew 18:21–22; Proverbs 3:5–6

Tool, Toy, or Tangent?

Karen Ehman

My times are in your hands;
deliver me from the hands of my enemies,
from those who pursue me.

(PSALM 31:15)

I have a love/hate relationship with social media: Facebook, Twitter, Pinterest, etc. I love how they keep me connected to family and friends, and how they enable me to spy on ... er, *keep up with* my kids. It's great to be able to quickly post a prayer request when accidents or sicknesses occur, and I love reconnecting with friends from my past.

But I hate the way social media can become a black hole, eating up time and energy while diverting my attention from what's most important. I can get lost in reading trivial posts or worse, caught up in the drama of heated opinion slinging that often occurs on the screen. As a result, I waste time.

As a guideline, I ask myself, is this a *tool*, a *toy*, or a *tangent*?

The Internet in general is a fabulous *tool*. It can be used for God and for good — organizing meals for a hurting family or participating in an online Bible study. But it can also be used for bad — cyberbullying, extramarital affairs, and airing frustrations.

It can also be a *toy*. Nothing wrong with toys. We all need a little fun and relaxation. And if we enjoy playing games online, that's great.

What crosses the line is when any online activity becomes a *tangent*: a sudden diversion that takes us off track from our priorities and responsibilities. Tangents torch our time, sap our strength, and can cause us to ignore loved ones. Tangents give us a false sense of being productive when, in reality, we aren't accomplishing anything. Then we feel frustrated, defeated, and even guilty about how much time we've wasted.

The psalmist placed his time in God's hands and asked for deliverance from his enemies (Psalm 31:15). Although he was speaking of enemies who could do him physical harm, we need to realize our tools, toys, and tangents have the potential to harm us too. I've had my own tangents that led me off track and caused me to neglect my family and responsibilities. This made me feel like a failure.

Maybe you have too. When you're engaging with social media today, prayerfully and carefully (with *all* honesty) ask yourself, "Am I using this as a tool, a toy, or a tangent?" By doing this and setting healthy boundaries, we can overcome the enemy of self-defeating behaviors and eliminate frustration. We can free up time for the important relationships and tasks God has for us and live our lives in a meaningful, not frivolous, way.

Dear Lord, teach me to use my time wisely, in ways that honor You and don't become tangents. I want to be efficient and effective for Your kingdom's work. In Jesus' name, Amen.

REMEMBER

When faced with an activity that could divert your attention or siphon your time, evaluate honestly whether at that particular time that pursuit is a tool, toy, or tangent.

REFLECT

How can you tell when you are wasting time on a tangent? When you sense this is happening, what should you do?

RESPOND

Make a list of things that can morph from a tool to a toy, or perhaps even become a tangent. Now, brainstorm ways to keep those activities in check. Can you set time limits? Solicit a friend to hold you accountable? Take a social media fast to realign your perspective?

POWER VERSES

Ecclesiastes 8:5–6; Ecclesiastes 12:13–14

Letters to Pastors

Lysa TerKeurst

Now we ask you, brothers and sisters,
to acknowledge those who work hard among you,
who care for you in the Lord and who admonish you.
Hold them in the highest regard in love because of their work.
Live in peace with each other.
(1 THESSALONIANS 5:12–13)

I recently shared part of my story during the weekend services at my home church. It was one of the biggest honors of my life. And my biggest takeaway? I don't know how pastors do it. Honest to goodness, I don't.

Sitting in the front row as the worship song concluded and the moment drew closer for me to step on stage, my heart became more and more desperate for Jesus to come back. Right now. *Rapture? Hello? God? Please?*

But no rapture came. And soon there I was in front of my home church, sweating like a toad on a hot tin roof. If toads sweat. I have no idea. And I'm way too tired to Google it. Anyhow.

Even though I speak for a living, there is something very different about speaking at my home church. I felt a weight of responsibility. I felt it in my heart. I felt it in my soul. I felt it in my brain.

And I thought to myself: *How does my pastor do this every week?* How does he craft a new sermon, get comfortable with that completely new material, carry the weight of responsibility, feel the anxiety of walking up on that platform, deliver a timed message in tune with the Holy Spirit, and then do it in multiple services during that same weekend? And. Then. Do. It. All. Again. Next. Weekend.

Seriously.

And when I was finished speaking, I sat down and decided I was going to write my pastor a letter. A letter to tell him how much I appreciate what he does and how much he sacrifices each and every week.

So I was thinking, maybe this would be a good thing for us to do together. Let's pull out a piece of stationery or a card, and write our pastor some words of encouragement in a thank-you note. And if we happen to know what the pastor's favorite restaurant is, and we're able, let's send along a gift card so our pastor can take his or her spouse out for dinner. Spouses carry the weight too. In a big way. As a matter of fact, let's write them a note of thanks as well.

Just as Paul urged the Thessalonians to esteem those working for the Lord, might I encourage you to do so today? Our pastors and their spouses work hard each week. Let's send a little love their way!

Dear Lord, thank You for the gift You've given my pastor to teach and preach Your precious Word. Please show me specific ways to encourage my pastor today. In Jesus' name, Amen.

REMEMBER

Esteem those working for the Lord.

REFLECT

When it comes to how you think about your pastor and his or her spouse, do you ever think/speak critical thoughts? What would change in your church experience if you instead chose to pray encouraging prayers for them?

RESPOND

Write your pastor a thank-you note today.

POWER VERSES

Hebrews 3:13; 1 Timothy 5:17

The Invisible Battle

Tracie Miles

Take the helmet of salvation and the sword of the Spirit,
which is the word of God.

(EPHESIANS 6:17)

It was a dream.

I was in a field in the middle of the night. Only moonbeams pierced the dark. Out of nowhere, unseen forces pressed me to the ground. Hatred spewed from the invisible evil. Fear encompassed me. I sensed God whispering that His Word was my only hope. I knew His truths held power over this wickedness.

As could only happen in a dream, I suddenly shrunk to the size of a pencil. I threw myself onto an open Bible, grabbed a handful of pages, and rolled. The papers tore from the binding as I wrapped myself tightly in God's Word. Instantly, the enemies retreated.

I woke up to my rapid heartbeat and the 3:00 a.m. blackness. My thoughts stumbled over one another. Although I knew I was safe in my own bed, my heart was ravaged by the battle in my dream. I spent the next hour talking with Jesus. The fears, hurts, and longings of my heart overflowed. After a while, a sense of peace washed over me — one I hadn't experienced in a long time.

You see, my family and I had been engaged in fierce spiritual warfare. The past year had been marked by harsh blows. Instead of naming it for what it was, I'd attributed the onslaught of hardships to "life." Through the dream, God showed me that we were under oppression. He helped me see I'd been trudging through life unknowingly carrying the crushing weight of disappointment, resentment, and stress.

Negative emotions that stemmed from being hurt by someone I loved, family concerns, as well as discouragement about our circumstances had erected a barrier between God and me. I'd grown weary of praying prayers that seemed to go unheard. Feelings overshadowed faith. And I'd been handling these adversities alone, rather than seeking God's wisdom. As a result, I'd given the devil a foothold. Devoting so much time to focusing on my circumstances and feelings had inadvertently minimized the time I spent focusing on God's Word.

Although I felt alone, God had never left my side. Deep down I knew that only He had the power to release me from my oppression. Through the dream, God helped me to see I had not been using the right weapons to fight this battle. His sword—the Bible—was what I needed to deliver me from the oppression, just as Ephesians 6:17 affirms.

Victory can only be found by spending time with Jesus and choosing His Word as our weapon. God never leaves us to fight battles alone. His Word tells us many times that the battle is His, but we must choose to wrap ourselves in His truth and believe He's our protector who will fight to the death for His children.

In fact, He already has.

Dear Lord, set me free from the grip the enemy has on my heart. Forgive me for thinking I could fight this battle on my own. When I am afraid, help me to wrap myself in Your Word. In Jesus' name, Amen.

REMEMBER

Spiritual warfare is real. Equipping yourself with the sword of God, His Word, is the weapon that will help you fight strongly in faith against the unseen enemy.

REFLECT

Could the weight of spiritual warfare be the cause of any oppression you've been feeling recently? What part of the armor of God covers the oppression you're under?

RESPOND

In what new ways can you begin wrapping yourself in God's Word and protecting yourself in this battle between good and evil? Pick a practice or two (memorizing Scripture or praying it, for example) and weave it into your daily routine.

POWER VERSES

Ephesians 6:13–18; Proverbs 4:23

Always Pray (And Don't Give Up)

Rachel Olsen

*Then Jesus told his disciples a parable to show them
that they should always pray and not give up.*

(LUKE 18:1)

Bam-bam … bam, bam-bam-bam …

The noise slowly fills my consciousness.

What is that?

I rub my eyes and glance at the clock on the nightstand: 5:51 a.m.

*Sounds like … hammering. Who's hammering at 6 o'clock in the morning—
on a Saturday?*

I get up and peer through the blinds to look into my neighbor's back-
yard. I'm not sure what I expect to see or what I think I might do about
it. If I see my neighbor hammering, am I really prepared to walk out there
—pink jammies, tousled hair, and all—and say something about poor
timing? I'm not very confrontational. But neither am I a morning person,
and this hammering has got to stop.

Bam-bam-bam … bam … bam-bam …

I wake my husband, Rick, with my movement at the window, the
rising sunlight breaking into the bedroom.

"Do you hear that noise?" I ask him. "*What* is that? It sounds like
hammering!"

Rick listens for a moment. "It's a woodpecker," he states with confidence. Anticipating my response, he adds, "You can't stop him."

I can't stop him? This sounds like a challenge. As Rick drifts back to
sleep, I head outside to find this bird. I spot it hanging off the side of my
house, pecking holes into the wood trim.

I try scaring it away. I scream at it. I throw sticks toward it. Don't
worry, animal lovers, I throw like a girl. It turns out Rick is right; I can't
stop the bird.

The woodpecker kept hammering, and I continued my antics. The
woodpecker remained undeterred. Occasionally, he'd fly off to a neigh-
boring tree only to fly back and peck the side of my house again as soon

as I'd gone back inside and tried to return to my pillow. So I finally gave up and granted him the right to hammer the house in peace. It's not what I wanted to do, but he wore me down. He was unstoppable.

Interestingly enough, Jesus told a story of a woman who had woodpecker-like faith. Woodpecker-like persistence. You just couldn't stop her. With the parable in Luke 18:1–8, Jesus taught His disciples to always pray and never give up. The woman in the parable petitioned a judge for justice so often and so boldly that he thought she would soon wear him out.

I wonder, do we constantly seek God with the same tenacity, asking Him in faith for what we need?

Jesus didn't describe the judge in this way to portray God as unwilling or easily exhausted by our requests — the judge doesn't represent God in this story. Jesus was saying: if an unjust judge would eventually grant the request of this woman, how much more will our gracious Father grant the requests of His own children?

God is willing to answer — to help, to restore, to vindicate, and redeem. But we must have faith. And we must ask Him. Sometimes — oftentimes — repeatedly. We need the kind of faith that will not give up. The kind of faith that just cannot be stopped. The kind of faith that prays *always*.

We need woodpecker faith.

Dear Lord, hear my prayers today about _____.
Thank You in advance for Your answers. In Jesus' name, Amen.

REMEMBER

Jesus wants you to pray with persistence.

REFLECT

What prayer would you like answered? What injustice do you need righted?

RESPOND

Set a reminder — on your phone, calendar, or on a sticky note — to pray for this four times in the next twenty-four hours.

POWER VERSES

Mark 9:23; James 5:13

The Opinion Blender

Amy Carroll

The words of the reckless pierce like swords,
but the tongue of the wise brings healing.
(PROVERBS 12:18)

I stood in shock after the first women's ministry event I coordinated several years ago. It seemed I was the hero of the day, and I couldn't take it all in. I looked at my friend Peggy and said, "I've no idea what to do with all the praise."

She smiled wickedly. "Don't worry," she said, "the criticism's coming."

She was right.

When in leadership of *any* kind — pastor, women's ministry director, mother, executive — you'll be thrown into a world of conflicting opinions. They'll swirl you around like a blender. If you're not careful, they'll spin you silly, puree your self-confidence, and leave you a soupy mess.

I once heard a pastor say that leaders have foes and fans but not many friends. When I received feedback about that first women's ministry event, it varied from constructive criticism to harsh critiques to sweet compliments. Talk about leaving me spinning! In the years since, I've gained some wisdom that has helped me navigate the opinion blender with insight and grace.

Dealing with criticism. Criticism is difficult to receive sometimes, but openness to it is essential for growth. However, I've found it's helpful to sift through criticism carefully instead of embracing each reproach fully. I weigh each one with two questions: "Is it true?" and "Is it helpful?" The criticism that is helpful and true most often comes from trusted people in my life. I surround myself with truth-telling friends who love me despite my flaws, but who also refuse to diminish those flaws. My friends don't shrink back from telling the truth, but they do stir love and kindness into the hard things I need to hear. They celebrate my successes and mourn my defeats.

Processing praise. Corrie ten Boom passed on her secret to receiving praise. To paraphrase: "I take each compliment as a flower, and at the

112

end of the day, I give the bouquet to Jesus." Her advice has helped me respond to praise. Because I want to respect the giver without seeming flippant, I'm not comfortable saying, "Give Jesus all the glory" when someone says something nice. But I *want* Jesus to get all the glory. I simply say "thank you" and gratefully receive the flower of praise. At the end of the day, I gather each compliment and give the bouquet to Jesus in prayer. It's a joy to return to Jesus what is His, and it's a sure way to hit the "stop" button on the opinion blender.

If you're in leadership, remember: You're not as bad as your foes say. You're not as wonderful as your fans say. The truth is somewhere in between.

Learning to receive helpful criticism is part of growth. Welcoming praise as encouragement and passing the compliment along to Jesus helps calm the whirl of the opinion blender. Both help us to remember we're loved servants of God on a journey to being like Jesus.

Dear Lord, help me find the balance of truth when receiving criticism and praise. I want to learn from legitimate criticism and return the praise to You. In Jesus' name, Amen.

REMEMBER

Both criticism and praise can be vehicles of personal growth if received with openness and the resolve to give God glory.

REFLECT

Who has earned the right to tell you hard truths? How do you respond to them?

RESPOND

Write down one criticism and one praise you've received in the past week. Consider the growth potential of the criticism (is it true? is it helpful?) and offer the praise back to Jesus.

POWER VERSES

Proverbs 15:12; Proverbs 15:31

Lost

T. Suzanne Eller

"Or suppose a woman has ten silver coins and loses one. Doesn't she light a lamp, sweep the house and search carefully until she finds it? And when she finds it, she calls her friends and neighbors together and says, 'Rejoice with me; I have found my lost coin.' In the same way, I tell you, there is rejoicing in the presence of the angels of God over one sinner who repents."

(LUKE 15:8–10)

I was awash in a sea of three toddlers. Trying to do anything outside the house was an adventure. But one day I decided to brave a trip to the mall to shop for Christmas gifts. As I stood at the register, I asked my children to hold onto mama's jeans. Their tightly clutched fists let me know that they were close. After completing my purchase, I turned around and realized that two-year-old Ryan was nowhere in sight. The three tiny hands clutching my pant leg turned out to be one child holding on with two hands, and the other holding on with one while their brother made his escape.

I buckled the kids in the monster-size stroller, threw my package underneath, and blasted through the store calling out my two-year-old's name.

"Have you seen my son? He's two. He has brown hair and he's tall for his age. Has anyone seen him?"

Finally an older woman approached me. "Honey, I saw a little boy with brown hair just a few moments ago carrying a really large box out those doors."

Seconds later, I saw him strolling through the mall with his little two-year-old gait, carrying an extra large shoebox. My son wasn't just lost. He had shoplifted a pair of men's shoes in the process.

I scooped up my little lost shoplifter and held him close.

Something had captured my toddler's attention and he had wandered. I knew what might have easily happened to him if I had not found him. My love for him meant I'd push that stroller to the ends of the earth, calling his name, until he was safe in my arms.

In his book *Amazing Grace*, K. W. Osbeck says, "If the New Testament teaches us anything, it teaches us about God's love in searching for lost men. Becoming a Christian in a very real sense is simply putting ourselves in the way of being found by God—to stop running from His loving pursuit."

Maybe you have escaped God. One adventure took you to the next and suddenly you were lost in a crowd, wondering if you'd gone too far.

You haven't.

Stop. Right where you are. Let Him scoop you up.

And that box of things you're carrying—those emotions, mistakes, choices you wish you'd never made—give it to Him. He'll return them to where they rightfully belong as He leads you back home.

Dear Lord, I willingly climb into Your arms. Please accept this box
of gathered mistakes and failures. Today I am joyfully found by You.
In Jesus' name, Amen.

REMEMBER

Stop. Right where you are. Empty your arms of that weight you've been carrying and lift it up to be scooped into your heavenly Father's embrace.

REFLECT

Name one way you've been running. What would it look like to stop?

RESPOND

Imagine God scooping you up as the woman in the parable scooped up her lost coin. Write down God's response to finding you as well as your response to being found by God.

POWER VERSES

Psalm 145:18–19; Psalm 119:151

When My Mean Girl Wants to Come Out

Lysa TerKeurst

"I have told you this so that my joy may be in you
and that your joy may be complete."
(JOHN 15:11)

Do you ever have days where someone tries to rip the joy right out of your life? I do. And it's really hard. The good girl part of my brain says, *Be nice. Honor Jesus with your actions. Your response is your responsibility. Self-control, Lysa, self-control.*

But the mean girl part of my brain says, *How dare they act that way! I'll show them!*

Issues.

I have them. Maybe most of us do. Especially that one special week a month.

But God.

I love how those two words interrupt me. Redirect me. Remind me. Comfort me. Battle the mean girl in me. And cause me to pause.

Pause. Just for a minute. And it's in that pause where we give the Holy Spirit room to interrupt the mean girl response just dying to come out. The Holy Spirit says, *Lysa, stop and think. It might feel good in the minute to scream, retaliate, pitch a fit, and flood the situation with scary emotions. But it won't feel good in the long run. You'll feel the sting of regret. Come on, Lysa, be rare. Be a girl who looks ahead and determines to do what's best in the long run.*

Yes, it stinks that this other person is determined to steal our joy. But in reality, our joy can only be stolen if we let it.

Jesus says, "If you keep my commands, you will remain in my love, just as I have kept my Father's commands and remain in his love. I have told you this so that my joy may be in you and that your joy may be complete. My command is this: Love each other as I have loved you" (John 15:10–12).

Several things struck me as I read this verse. Any time I interact with others, I'm faced with the choice to remain in God's love or retreat from God's love. I can't control how someone is acting toward me, but I *can* control how I act and react. If I choose to remain in God's love and react to this other person kindly, it affects my joy.

Jesus interjects His joy right into the heart of a kind person. If I choose to be kind, instead of my joy being depleted, it will be completed.

So back off, mean girl part of my brain. The Jesus girl in me is taking over—and holding on to every ounce of joy that's rightfully mine. Circumstances can steal stuff from me. But not my joy.

Dear Lord, this sounds so good in this moment. But it will not be easy when I interact with that person who makes my mean girl want to come out. Will You help me remember these truths? And help me remember if I react kindly, my joy can be completed rather than depleted. In Jesus' name, Amen.

REMEMBER

Circumstances can steal stuff, but not joy.

REFLECT

What would it be like to live with Jesus' complete joy in your heart?

RESPOND

Choose a relationship in which your mean girl often comes out. Think of three specific ways it would look to *retreat from* God's love when your joy is tested. (For example, you become grumpy, say harsh words, and throw things across the room.) Now, think of three specific ways it would look to *remain in* God's love. (For example, you use a kind tone, choose to believe the best of that person, or do them a favor.)

POWER VERSES

John 15:10, 12; Hebrews 12:2

Sacrificial Love

Samantha Evilsizer

*"You lack one thing: go, sell all that you have and give to the poor,
and you will have treasure in heaven; and come, follow me."*
(MARK 10:21 ESV)

I had some misplaced priorities. I suppose at some level I'd known it for some time. But I didn't fully recognize how misplaced they were until I took a trip to El Salvador with a Christian humanitarian organization.

I met two children on a home visit. They lifted their tarp door and invited me into mud puddles and dirt walls with just one bed where their family of five rested at night. One bed for dreaming dreams of being a doctor and a police officer.

I'd come to offer gifts of detergent and food. But the children's gifts exceeded anything I had to give. A tiny beaded bracelet smudged with dirt, drenched in love. They wanted it to be mine. They filled my hands with selfless love. Love shared in smiles and what few tangible gifts they owned.

Feeling too shy to hand me the bracelet herself, the girl nudged her brother. He presented it to me as if it were a royal crown and slid it gently on my wrist. I declare, diamonds couldn't match the worth of their hearts, their gift in that moment.

The next morning as I was getting dressed, I felt a nudge. *Give your bracelet away like those children gave theirs to you.*

You see, I had another precious bracelet with me. It was one my dad had given me over twenty years ago. Just a simple wooden bracelet from South Africa, but it meant the world to me.

How could I part with it? I wrestled with indecision. My heart soared, anticipating the moment I'd spot a mama to whom I would give my bracelet. Then my heart sank, anxious at the thought of giving up one of my treasures.

And there lay the problem. My misplaced treasure.

I'm embarrassed ... heartbroken. I'm sad to say I couldn't give it away.

Couldn't? No; more like I *wouldn't*. Both bracelets journeyed back home with me. One bearing selflessness; the other, selfishness.

I thought I was really something, bringing gifts to those kids in the form of beans and rice. Little did I know, I was the one in need. I needed God's mercy. I needed a new perspective. I don't want possessions if I'm not willing to use them to love others.

I needed the one thing I lacked ... more love for the Lord than for my possessions. My heart held tighter to my bracelet than it did to what God had asked me to do. He beckoned, "Give to the poor, and you will have treasure in heaven." A simple request, yet so difficult to follow.

I don't want to be lacking in love for the Lord or those He cares for. Next time, I'm giving it all. I'm starting by opening my hands and heart and looking for opportunities today. Are you with me?

Dear Lord, You are the perfect example of giving. Thank You for new mercies, second chances, and a heart capable of responding to Your prompting. Help me to respond to Your prompting this day. In Jesus' name, Amen.

REMEMBER

You need more love for the Lord than for your possessions.

REFLECT

You can choose each day to bear selflessness or selfishness. Why is it sometimes easier to hold more tightly to earthly possessions?

RESPOND

Set up a time to volunteer with those who have less than you to help gain perspective on what's important.

POWER VERSES

Matthew 6:20; 1 Timothy 6:18–19

Do I Have Father Issues?

Glynnis Whitwer

> *"Are not two sparrows sold for a penny?*
> *Yet not one of them will fall to the ground*
> *outside your Father's care."*
>
> (MATTHEW 10:29)

My friend's father abandoned the family when she was young. As a result, she struggled with relating to God as her Father. Another friend's dad was harsh and critical. It took years for her to feel unconditionally loved by God.

As a young believer, I didn't think I had issues with my father. My father was a good man, hardworking, and faithful to his family. But he was an uninvolved presence in my life. If I had a problem, I went to my mother. If I got into trouble, I called my mother. When I wanted advice, well, you can guess who I approached.

For years, I congratulated myself on navigating my father's distant personality with minimal negative impact. Then, ten years ago, I heard that everyone (even those with great dads) has some kind of "father issue" with God because of our human earthly fathers.

Could it be true for me? Was something missing in my relationship with God because of my relationship with my dad? As I dug deep, I discovered that although I was confident of God's love, I didn't really trust Him to be there in times of trouble. Would He step in if I had a problem? Did He truly care about me?

Every question revealed the same disturbing truth: I didn't *really* trust God. Believe in? Yes. Love? Yes. But trust? The words were easy to say, but my heart wasn't in them.

This realization shed light on so many issues that hadn't seemed troublesome enough to address. Like why I had trouble praying for myself, why fear controlled me at times, and why I neglected to seek God's wisdom in decision making.

It seems I really did have father issues that were affecting my intimacy with God. I didn't know what it was like to have a father to turn to in good or bad times. But I desperately wanted to.

As awkward as it felt, I decided to make some changes. I was intentional about being more personal in prayer, even addressing God as "Daddy" (*Abba*, Mark 14:36). Faced with decisions, I asked God for advice (James 1:5). And when fear started to well up, I declared my trust in God despite my emotions.

Little by little, my faith and trust grew. I took doubtful thoughts captive and intentionally exchanged them with thoughts that affirmed God's trustworthiness to help in times of trouble. It took years to rewire my thinking with the truth about God's ability and willingness to be my heavenly Father. And honestly, I'm still a work in progress.

When I slip back into my independent ways, I choose to believe what I know to be true: I have a heavenly Daddy who wants to be my hero, champion, protector, and confidant—if I'll only let Him.

Dear heavenly Father, You are perfect in all Your ways. Your Word says You are a loving Father, and I long to know You in that way. Only You know the gaps in our relationship based on my imperfect understanding of You. Please help me work through them. In Jesus' name, Amen.

REMEMBER

Your relationship with your earthly father often affects your relationship with your heavenly Father. It's your responsibility to believe the truth about God's character based on His Word.

REFLECT

How does your relationship with your earthly father impact your relationship with your heavenly Father?

RESPOND

What do you wish were different in your relationship with God? Do you wish you trusted Him more or accepted His unconditional love? Commit this week to pray as if you believed that wish to be true, and watch God respond.

POWER VERSES

Matthew 6:26; Psalm 91:14–15

Lord, I Need Your Help

Renee Swope

In my distress I called to the LORD;
I cried to my God for help.

(PSALM 18:6)

One evening after an intense "discussion," my husband, JJ, told me that no matter what he did or how hard he tried, it was never enough for me. He was right. I constantly found fault with him as a husband and as a dad.

But when he implied that I was impossible to please ... well, that sent my already-out-of-control emotions reeling. I grabbed my coat and stormed out the front door. Hot tears streamed down my cheeks as I replayed our conversation in my head.

I was determined to figure out what JJ's problem was and get Jesus to fix him. So I started filing complaints against my husband in what you might call a prayer. And I finally heard myself—all the ugliness, all the anger. That's when I realized, *I need help.* I needed God to help me figure out how—after seven years of a happy marriage—we had gotten to this ugly place.

Instead of just crying, I found myself *crying out* to God for help.

King David was much better at this than I was that day. He had a habit of crying out to God for help when he was in distress. One Bible scholar notes that the phrase, " 'In my distress' refers, most probably, not to any particular case, but rather indicates [David's] general habit of mind, that when he was in deep distress and danger he had uniformly called upon the Lord, and had found him ready to help."*

That night, when I stopped talking and started listening, I sensed God showing me I wanted JJ to make up for all the ways my dad had fallen short as a father to me and as a husband to my mom. Years as a child in a broken home with a broken heart had led to a significant sense of loss and deep disappointment. Yet, up to that point, I had never grieved the happily-ever-after that I longed for but didn't have.

---

*Albert Barnes, *Barnes' Notes on the Old and New Testaments* (Grand Rapids: Baker, 1983), accessed online at http://bible.cc.psalm/18-6.htm.

My unfulfilled hopes had become bitter expectations. I became controlling and critical, thinking that if I could get JJ to be the husband and dad I wanted him to be, maybe my broken dreams could be put back together. But I was wrong. Instead of expecting my husband to make up for my losses, I needed to cry out to God with my hurts and call on Him for help.

Are there hurts that hold you hostage? Expectations no one could really ever meet? Need some help today? I know I do. And I know God is there, waiting for us to cry out to Him.

As I continued to process what had happened in my childhood and how it affected my marriage, I learned to ask God for help through each step of my healing journey. It took time, prayer, and courage, but God was my very present help.

By the way, I'm crazy about my husband. And so very thankful for that day several years ago when I finally asked the Lord for help.

Dear Lord, I need Your help, especially with _____.
Please show me where to start and be my help each step of the way.
In Jesus' name, Amen.

REMEMBER

Hurts from your past can hold you hostage. God is there, waiting to heal you.

REFLECT

In what ways do you file complaints against your husband (or other loved one) in what you might call a prayer?

RESPOND

Determine if your hurts are too deep to heal without outside help. If they are, consider seeing a pastor or counselor.

POWER VERSES

Psalm 46:1; Deuteronomy 4:7

Longing to Be Pursued

Lynn Cowell

"Since you are precious and honored in my sight,
and because I love you, I will give people in exchange for you,
nations in exchange for your life."
(ISAIAH 43:4)

My heart beats wildly. "Hurry, hurry! You'll be too late!"

I've watched this movie over and over. I know the hero will come to the rescue at the last second and demand, "She goes free!" to the captain. I know he'll risk his life to save hers.

It doesn't matter that I already know what will happen. The thrill of the pursuit and a heroic rescue sends my heart pounding every time.

I know I'm not alone. Countless women curl up on their couches to watch the same chick flicks time and again, especially the ones in which the hero gives everything to save the girl. Like the women rescued in movies, we want to be desired, fought for, pursued. And we are.

Our Creator Himself pursues us, but it's so much better than in the movies. He gave up His life and paid a great price to rescue us.

Certainly, there had been many times I had seen Jesus as my Savior, Shepherd, and Friend. But it wasn't until I read this passage from Isaiah that I fully realized how valuable I am to Him:

> "Don't be afraid, I've redeemed you. I've called your name. You're mine. When you're in over your head, I'll be there with you. When you're in rough waters, you will not go down. When you're between a rock and a hard place, it won't be a dead end—
>
> "Because I am GOD, your personal God, The Holy of Israel, your Savior. I paid a huge price for you: all of Egypt, with rich Cush and Seba thrown in! *That's* how much you mean to me! That's how much I love you! I'd sell off the whole world to get you back, trade the creation just for you" (Isaiah 43:1–4 MSG).

He'd give up everything just for me? That's crazy! But that's the radical love that revolutionized my life. When I read these verses, I began to

124

see a side of Jesus I'd never seen. He pursues me. He loves me more than anything. And He wants to be my everything.

This truth satisfied a deep longing I didn't know I had. This is the love that fills my wanting heart and settles the question, *Am I valuable enough to be pursued?*

Yes, I am. And so are you.

Dear Lord, I know You created this part of me that wants to be pursued and rescued. I know I am designed to be filled only by Your unconditional love. Thank You that You will never grow tired of me or stop pursuing me. In Jesus' name, Amen.

REMEMBER

No man, dad, boyfriend, or husband can fully fill the love gap in our hearts to be pursued. Only the One who created your heart can: Jesus.

REFLECT

What indicators do you see in your life that reveal your need to be pursued and fought for?

RESPOND

Write out Psalm 45:11 (MSG), putting in your name: "The king is wild for _____." When you feel rejected, remind yourself of this truth—your King is crazy for you!

Think of a time when you did not feel wanted or pursued. Rewrite that story, this time with Jesus there to fill that rejection and vulnerability. Whenever the memory comes back, replace it with the truth that God would trade the whole world for you!

POWER VERSES

John 3:16; Zephaniah 3:17

Asking God for the Impossible

Lysa TerKeurst

"I will go before you and will level the mountains;
I will break down gates of bronze and cut through bars of iron.
I will give you hidden treasures, riches stored in secret places,
so that you may know I am the LORD, the God of Israel,
who summons you by name."

(ISAIAH 45:2–3)

Several years ago, I sat beside my youngest sister and listened as she boldly rejected my views of God. She told me how she'd always been a free spirit, much too unconventional for traditional religion.

"Good thing I'm not into religion," I gently replied.

She twisted her face as if half expecting a lightning bolt to strike us both. "But you *are* religious," she said.

I laid my head against the back of the lounge chair, closed my eyes to the sun now washing over me, and simply replied, "Nope."

Letting my statement just sit for a while, I decided not to clarify unless she asked. And ask she did.

That's when I explained that I follow God, not a list of rules. I am passionate about getting into the Bible—God's teachings—and letting the Bible get into me. I no longer evaluate life based on my feelings. Instead, I let my feelings and experiences be evaluated in light of God's Word.

I have watched God chase me around with rich evidence of His presence and invitations to trade apathy for active faith. But I had to make the choice to see God. Hear God. Know God. And follow hard after God.

Then I took my sister's hand and told her I'd be praying for God to mess with her in ways too bold for her to deny.

Fast forward over six years later. My sister walks into her professor's office and sees one of my books on the bookshelf. I don't think she really believed anyone actually read my books. But there it was. And it messed with her.

She later went home and poked around my blog a bit, where she found a clip of my testimony. Again, it messed with her. One verse in particular messed with her so much that she let the possibility that God exists slip into her heart.

A few days later, she went and had "Jeremiah 29:11" tattooed on the back of her neck, which is the reference for this promise: " 'For I know the plans I have for you,' declares the LORD, 'plans to prosper you and not to harm you, plans to give you hope and a future.' " And she started calling, wanting to talk to me. About life. About tattoos. And about God.

A few weeks after she got the tattoo, I stood in the middle of an airport praying for my precious sister who called while I was traveling, and asked me to pray for her. She had called. She had asked. And that's the miracle of our Jesus. He is the God of the impossible.

I wonder what might happen if we dared to ask God for the impossible just a little more often. I'm up for it. Are you?

Dear Lord, use me today to reach the heart of one. I want to trade any apathy I may have for active faith. Lead me, and I will follow. In Jesus' name, Amen.

REMEMBER

The miracle of our Jesus is He is the God of the impossible.

REFLECT

What intrigues you about knowing nothing is impossible for God to do and no one is impossible for God to reach?

RESPOND

Take a few moments to wonder what might happen if you dared to ask God for the impossible just a little more often.

POWER VERSES

John 15:13; Ephesians 1:17

The Honeymoon Life

Sharon Glasgow

Strength and honour are her clothing;
and she shall rejoice in time to come.
(PROVERBS 31:25 KJV)

My heart sank as she told me the tragic end to her love story. When she and her husband married, they couldn't afford a nice honeymoon. Kids soon followed and the money to do something special together just never seemed to be there.

When their last child was leaving for college, they finally made arrangements for their perfect honeymoon. Then her husband was tragically killed in a car accident before they left. Her dreams were shattered.

Her story affected me deeply. Although my husband was still alive, I hadn't had the honeymoon of my dreams either. On our wedding night, we stayed at a state park. For years, I too dreamed of a "real" honeymoon. But after hearing my friend's story, I changed my thinking.

Rather than a honeymoon trip, I wanted a honeymoon life.

In prayer, I made this commitment to the Lord: *My husband is Yours. I don't know how long my days with him will be. But I trust You to teach me how to spend our time wisely. When our days are done, I don't want to have any regrets. Teach me how to be a lover of You first. And by loving You, I will know how to love my husband fully—especially when the days are hard, the storms rage, and the sun sets at the close of our life together on earth.*

The Lord gave me peace. And this verse came to mind: "Strength and honour are her clothing; and she shall rejoice in time to come" (Proverbs 31:25 KJV).

I knew God was telling me to not be afraid of what tomorrow might bring. He would give me the strength to live the honeymoon life successfully and married life to the fullest.

A few weeks later, my husband and I celebrated our anniversary. We couldn't afford a special trip, but that didn't discourage me. This was the start of our honeymoon life. I packed a picnic of his favorite foods and we enjoyed the meal, and each other, in the middle of the field behind our house. No trip around the world, no lavish hotel, no gourmet dish could surpass the gift of our time in that field and the way God changed my perspective.

I've chosen to live the honeymoon life every day. I cherish the simple things, like making my husband's favorite dishes, going to bed at the same time, and praying together. I even enjoy our mundane trips to the store together.

We've been living the honeymoon life for sixteen years now and have been married for thirty-one. With God's help, I've been able to see every day as an opportunity to love my husband in a special way. We may never go on that honeymoon trip, but I'll take a picnic in a field any day.

Lord, give me the ability to live the honeymoon life with my husband. Help me to stop focusing on the what if's of the future and to start focusing on loving to the fullest today. In Jesus' name, Amen.

REMEMBER

It isn't trips, diamonds, or flowers that make a marriage. It's how you live married life every day that makes it romantic and priceless.

REFLECT

What excites you about living every day as if it were your last with your husband? Do you love him outrageously as no one else could?

RESPOND

If you've fallen out of love, fall in love again. Let your actions every day—big or small—tell him there is none better than he. Love him intimately. Listen to him intently. Never be too tired to help lift him up when he is down. Make yourself and your home a sanctuary of loveliness.

POWER VERSES

Proverbs 31:10–11; Hebrews 10:24

When You Can't See
What God Is Building

Tracie Miles

For every house has a builder,
but the one who built everything is God.
(HEBREWS 3:4 NLT)

My son's social studies teacher assigned the task of making a pyramid. There were no specific criteria given about the size, or what materials to use—only that students rely on their imagination.

When Michael told me about his school project, I immediately put on my crafty-mom hat. *How much cardboard and hot glue would we need?* However, when he told his daddy about it, the project took on grander proportions. Before I knew it, we were at the hardware store.

"Lumber and nails?" I eyeballed my husband as if he had forgotten it was a seventh-grade project. He smiled and said, "I know."

I had no idea how a few 2 x 4s could be transformed into a pyramid. My husband, on the other hand, is a builder by trade, so he had a clear vision of the pyramid in our son's future.

He and Michael spent hours measuring and sawing and nailing. Step by step, a triangular form evolved. I watched and waited for my husband's vision to become a reality—and when it did, it truly was amazing!

As I marveled at this work of art, God spoke gentle reassurance to my soul. He knew my heart had been heavy, worried about several adversities and hardships my family was facing.

I'd been questioning His ways, wondering how He could bring good out of our difficult circumstances. God chose this moment to whisper to my spirit, *I am creating something good, beyond your human understanding. Trust Me as your Builder.*

Hebrews 3:4 quickly came to mind. There we are reminded that God is the builder of everything, including us. We are His temple, where His Holy Spirit resides. He's always at work building our lives so He can be glorified through us.

Here is what theologian Albert Barnes says about this passage: "Every family must have a founder; every dispensation an author; every house a builder. There must be someone, therefore, over all dispensations."* And that Someone is God.

The theological definition of the word *dispensation* is "the divine ordering of the affairs of the world; an appointment, arrangement, or favor, as by God." In other words, God is arranging and rearranging our lives in accordance with His will. Step by step, day by day, and with each circumstance we face. He is constructing a dwelling place for His presence within us.

What comfort it brings to know that in the same way my husband had a clear picture of what he planned to build, God has a vision of the masterpiece He is building in my life and in yours. Although we may not understand or like the building process, we can trust our Builder and know that He is looking out for our best.

Dear Lord, I trust You are doing a good work in me. Help me embrace the promise that You are building my life based on Your beautiful design, even when I cannot envision the outcome. In Jesus' name, Amen.

REMEMBER

No matter what is going on in your life, God is building something wonderful according to His master plan.

REFLECT

In what areas have you been questioning God's design for your life or neglecting to fully trust that His ways are always right and good?

RESPOND

Consider making a historical timeline of your life, highlighting situations where you can see how God was faithful and at work even when you didn't know what He was up to at the time. Allow these examples of His faithfulness to help you build a new attitude of trust in Him.

POWER VERSES

Psalm 127:1; Psalm 139:13

---

*Albert Barnes, *Barnes' Notes on the Old and New Testaments* (Grand Rapids: Baker, 1983), accessed online at http://bible.cc.hebrews/3-4.htm.

When Your Mess Becomes Your Message

Micca Campbell

Heal me, LORD, and I will be healed;
save me and I will be saved, for you are the one I praise.
(JEREMIAH 17:14)

For twenty years, my brother was absent from our family because of drug addiction. Countless times, we thought he was dead; according to drug abuse statistics, he should have been. However, my brother is living proof that God is in the restoration business. It doesn't matter who you are, what you've done, or what has been done to you. God is willing and able to turn any tragedy into triumph.

After entering many treatment programs with hopes of success and end results of failure, my brother finally found the answer: Jesus. It wasn't until he met the Lord that he experienced lasting healing and life change. Suddenly, all things became new.

My brother didn't have the strength, willpower, or ability to free himself from bondage, but that changed when he surrendered his life to Christ. The same is true for us. No matter what the bondage is — drugs, lust, gluttony, pride, anger, or fear — until we renounce our sickness and surrender to Christ, we will never experience freedom. On the other hand, when we are willing to give King Jesus our mess, He turns it into our message. And that's exactly what happened to my brother. Not a day goes by that my brother doesn't look for opportunities to brag on God and share His message of hope.

Such an opportunity arose one evening when my sister, brother, and I met together for dinner at a local restaurant. Our server was twenty-six-year-old Tiffany. Right away, we noticed two things about Tiffany. She had a natural gift for putting people at ease, and she was very pregnant. While we enjoyed her kind service, we had no idea that God would soon call us to serve her.

It started when my sister refused to allow my brother to pay for her dinner. While my sister loves to give to others, she's not so good at receiving. I, on the other hand, understood that it gave my brother great pleasure to pick up the check. The Lord knows I didn't want to deny him his blessing!

Poor Tiffany found herself caught in the middle. Eager to win her over to his side, my brother said to Tiffany, "You see, I was a drug addict for years. During that time, my sisters did a lot for me. Now, I just want to bless them."

Tiffany's eyes widened. "You were a drug addict?" she inquired. "I would have never guessed."

"Yes, I was," my brother replied. "But Jesus changed all that." Then he told Tiffany his life-changing story.

"I went from being lost to being found; from being homeless to being a homeowner; from being an employee to owning my own business; from being bound by drugs to being set free in Christ."

Tears filled Tiffany's eyes as we shared God's love with her. That's not all. Later that week, we confirmed God's love to her by presenting her with a gift for her baby.

When you and I—like my brother—allow God to turn our mess into our message, He not only changes our lives, but He changes the lives of others too.

Dear Lord, Your mercy astounds me. Give me opportunities to speak of Your hope so others may know Your goodness and salvation. In Jesus' name, Amen.

REMEMBER

No matter what your bondage, surrendering it to Christ is the pathway to freedom.

REFLECT

What steps do you need to take today to move from bondage to freedom? Reflect with gratitude on how God has turned your mess into a message that can encourage or bring life change to others.

RESPOND

Go for it! Write out your story of surrender and ask God to provide opportunities for you to encourage others.

POWER VERSES

Luke 19:10; Ephesians 2:8–9

When God Hurts Your Feelings

Lysa TerKeurst

I know what it is to be in need, and I know what it is to have plenty.
I have learned the secret of being content in any and every situation,
whether well fed or hungry, whether living in plenty or in want.
I can do all this through him who gives me strength.

(PHILIPPIANS 4:12–13)

Has God ever hurt your feelings? Honestly, sometimes these verses from Philippians are a tough pill to swallow.

Content in any and every situation? Really?

Several years ago, my daughter was a state champion gymnast. She was beautiful, graceful, and captivating to watch. One night while practicing for one of the largest tournaments she'd ever compete in, she fell. It was a move she'd done hundreds of times with the greatest of ease. But this time something went terribly wrong and that one mistake ended her gymnastic dreams.

We spent a year going from doctor to doctor only to be told she'd never be able to support the weight of her body on her injured shoulder again.

This was heart wrenching. Watching a fourteen-year-old girl wrestle with the fact that her dreams were stripped away doesn't exactly lend itself to feelings of contentment. Now, I know in the grand scheme of life, people face much worse situations. But in her world, this was huge. It was tempting to wallow and tell God He'd hurt our feelings.

Why did this happen?

Why didn't You stop this, God?

Why weren't my prayers answered?

Have you been there? Have you ever had a big situation in your life where you just couldn't process why God would allow it to happen? Or maybe even a small annoyance, like losing your keys on a morning you really needed to be somewhere?

It's so tempting to wallow in the why.

Asking why is perfectly normal. Asking why isn't unspiritual. However, if asking why pushes us farther from God rather than drawing us closer to Him, it is the wrong question.

If asking why doesn't offer hope, what will?

The *what* question.

In other words: *Now that this is my reality,* what *am I supposed to do with it?*

When I need to refocus my thinking from the *why* to the *what,* I rely on the apostle Paul's wisdom: "Whatever is true, whatever is noble, whatever is right, whatever is pure, whatever is lovely, whatever is admirable —if anything is excellent or praiseworthy—think about such things" (Philippians 4:8). I call this verse "directions on where to park my mind."

And that's exactly what Ashley has had to do with her dashed gymnastics dreams. Instead of wallowing in why this happened, I've had to help her ask:

This is my reality; now what am I going to do with it?

What can I learn from this?

What part of this is for my protection?

What other opportunities could God be providing?

What maturity could God be building into me?

Switching from the *why* to the *what* question paves the road to parking our minds in a much better place.

Is it easy? Nope. But is it a way to find perspective for situations we feel God has allowed into our lives that we don't understand and absolutely don't like? Yes.

Dear Lord, I know You love me. But sometimes it's just hard to understand the circumstances that come my way. I find myself consumed with trying to figure things out rather than looking for Your perspective and trusting You. Thank You for this new way to look at things. In Jesus' name, Amen.

REMEMBER

Switching from the *why* to the *what* question paves the road to parking your mind in a much better place.

REFLECT

Refocus your thinking from the *why* to the *what* by relying on the apostle Paul's wisdom: "Whatever is true, whatever is noble, whatever is right, whatever is pure, whatever is lovely, whatever is admirable—if anything is excellent or praiseworthy—think about such things" (Philippians 4:8).

RESPOND

Recall a recent experience that prompted you to ask the *why* question. Use the *what* questions from the devotion to park your mind in a better place by looking for the ways in which God may be teaching, protecting, providing for, and maturing you.

POWER VERSES

Isaiah 55:8–9; 2 Corinthians 10:5

A Simple Thank You

T. Suzanne Eller

Gracious words are like a honeycomb,
sweetness to the soul and health to the body.
(PROVERBS 16:24 ESV)

My girls once accused me of being the worst when it came to accepting a compliment.

"Mom, you look pretty today."

"Thanks, babe," I'd reply. "You're kind to say that when my hair is kind of crazy."

Or I'd give them the *You're just saying that* look.

Some might say it was self-effacing. Maybe even humble. But it wasn't either. It was a bad habit, one that sent a not-so-great message to my two beautiful daughters.

One day I heard my daughter do the same thing and it stopped me in my tracks. She was beautiful. Intelligent. Insightful. How could she turn a compliment into a negative?

Oh, yeah. She'd heard me do it.

From that day on, I made a conscious effort to change my words. And I began to listen to conversations among friends, women who were strong and beautiful. The conversations went something like this:

"Love those shoes." "Oh, these? Bought them on sale. Cheap as dirt."

"You did a great job on that lesson." "I was so nervous. Couldn't you tell?"

"You look nice." "Do you see this blemish? Right on my nose!"

Like a game of ping-pong, we often negate the good, bringing it down a notch … or two or three.

Saying thank you is a form of gratitude. Sure, it's acknowledging a compliment, but it's also accepting the thoughtful words of the person who spoke them.

But can we take this deeper?

Research shows a girl's self-worth takes a nosedive after the age of nine. It would be easy to point to a host of other factors, but what about us? What do our daughters and the other young women we influence hear us saying?

When someone offers a sincere compliment, what is your response? When someone acknowledges a trait they value in you, do you point out things you wish you could change about yourself?

It's been years since my daughters' words made me stop and think. They are grown and they are beautiful, but what I love best about them is the women they have become. I tell them often.

You are beautiful. I see God in you. I love the way you love others. And they simply say, "Thank you."

The next time someone gives you a compliment—whether it's as simple as, "Mom, those were great pancakes" or as kind as, "You're always so thoughtful"—receive it. You might want to point out the messy kitchen, or your bed head, or your not-so-gracious attitude instead, but someone sees something he or she likes in you and that's a gift.

Say it with me: *Thank you.*

Dear Lord, when someone stops long enough to say something kind,
help me offer a gracious reply. Help my words lift up those around me too.
In Jesus' name, Amen.

REMEMBER

There is a difference between self-deprecation and humility. One belittles who you are, while the other offers gracious security in Whose you are.

REFLECT

When someone gives you a compliment, how do you typically respond?

RESPOND

Make a pact with a friend or loved one to respond with a simple thank you to every compliment you receive today.

POWER VERSES

Proverbs 25:11; Colossians 4:6

Never Alone

Samantha Evilsizer

*"As the Father has loved me, so have I loved you. Now remain
in my love. If you keep my commands, you will remain in my love,
just as I have kept my Father's commands and remain in his love."*

(JOHN 15:9–10)

Miss Emma's wrinkled hands cupped my chin, her palm a reservoir for
my tears. I walked down the hallways saying tearless good-byes to 119
other nursing home residents, and yet my farewell to her released a levee
of pent-up emotions. I couldn't abandon her. It felt utterly wrong to leave
her alone, forsaken in this dark place.

My first "real" job at this institution—which my coworkers and I
referred to as "The Brick"—would have been bleak if not for Miss Emma
and a few others. Over the one year I worked there, I didn't allow many
details of this place to get beyond the surface of my heart. Yet one name,
one person, was chiseled there deeply: Miss Emma.

I perched on the edge of her bed, the edge of our good-bye, unable
to leave her. *Who'll sit in the sunshine with you? Who'll listen? Who'll sing
hymns with you?*

Visions of Miss Emma alone left me aching for her. But she was bright
with hope. Her beautiful brown eyes brimmed with confidence.

"I'll be fine, sugar," she said. "I'm never alone. Don't you realize the
One who created the sun sits with me? He listens always, hearing my
prayers and needs. His presence is in the very words we sing to Him.
Child, we're never alone."

Tucked away from the world, Miss Emma changed mine. She lived
securely rooted to the Vine. She read the words of Scripture and tethered
herself to Jesus' love through worship and prayer. Miss Emma lived in the
truth of St. Patrick's prayer: "Christ beside me, Christ before me, Christ
behind me, Christ within me, Christ beneath me, Christ above me."

Although she had been abandoned by her earthly family, she rested in
the knowledge that her heavenly Father never would leave her. Indeed,
He made a home in her so she could nestle in Him.

Might you rest in this comforting truth too? Curl up in His love by writing a Scripture verse on your heart. Lean into God's sure presence by lifting your voice in praise. Abide in His peace with prayer. Christ is within you, before you, behind you. And as Miss Emma so confidently knew, He will never leave or forsake you. You're never alone.

Dear Lord, thank You for making a home within me so I may rest secure in You. Because You are my dwelling place, I am never alone. In Jesus' name, Amen.

REMEMBER

Even if you are abandoned by your earthly family, you can rest in the knowledge that your heavenly Father never will leave. Indeed, He makes a home in you.

REFLECT

If you have been abandoned or rejected by others, how has this affected your trust level with God?

RESPOND

Spend time in God's presence today in one of these three ways: praise, prayer, or reading the Bible.

POWER VERSES

Deuteronomy 31:6; Matthew 28:20

Me and My Mama Mouth

Karen Ehman

She opens her mouth with wisdom,
and the teaching of kindness is on her tongue.
(PROVERBS 31:26 ESV)

The other day my son, a smart preteen, was up to the challenge of washing the dishes. He didn't give me an attitude when asked. He wasn't disrespectful. He didn't drag his feet. So why was I battling the urge to harshly point out how he was doing it all wrong?

Because he wasn't doing it my way.

He started with the grimy pots, then moved to the plates and silverware. Finally, he had to bubble up more water to spit-shine the glasses. While working, he stacked plastic cups in a pyramid.

Irritation welled up. An unkind reaction was itching to come out. I could easily have let my mama mouth take over: *It uses way more water to wash the dishes in that order. Plus the water is filthy now! Stop playing with those cups while you work. You're so slow.*

I wanted to be a control freak. I wanted to fire off the unkind words hidden in my unspoken thoughts: *The only way to do the dishes is my way. I see different as wrong. I interpret a preteen being a preteen—with a slight distraction of fun—as "slow."*

But any time I unload on Junior, or anyone, it has the potential to damage our relationship and plant seeds in his mind of his mom's view of him, whether verbalized or implied (lazy, wasteful, distracted, and slow). It does not, as Proverbs 31:26 (ESV) states, come close to resembling a woman who "opens her mouth with wisdom, and [speaks with] kindness on her tongue."

It's better if these scenarios go down differently. So let's replay that scene with a Spirit-controlled response.

As I see my son doing the dishes, I can make a mental note to explain how to do it next time in a way that will save water, money, and time. I can praise his efforts, keeping in mind his age and abilities. I can acknowledge his unique method: *I saw the clever way you stacked those dishes. You always make work fun.*

I can ask myself questions that will help keep my mama mouth in check. Questions like: *Does it matter now or will it matter tomorrow? Will it affect eternity? Is God trying to teach me something? Can I pause and praise instead of interrupt and instigate? Is this really an issue that needs addressing? Am I being a control freak? Do I need to let it go?*

The interaction wouldn't damage; it would nurture. It would be wise. Kind. And there would be no lost time, regrets, or need to call in the United Nations peacekeeping forces for intervention.

This mama would be less control-freakish and more Proverbs 31 womanish. It might not come easily—trust me, it usually doesn't—but with the Holy Spirit, it *is* possible to speak with kindness.

Dear Lord, may I purpose to temper my words with Your Holy Spirit as I interact with my family today. In Jesus' name, Amen.

REMEMBER

My mouth can be a powerful tool of encouragement or a weapon of destruction.

REFLECT

Which of the questions posed in the devotion (*Does it matter now or will it matter tomorrow?* etc.) do you most need to ask yourself when tempted to over-control?

RESPOND

Think of an incident from the past where you did not use your words in a way that was kind or loving. Revisit the situation. How could you have spoken in a way that would honor God? Could you have used a different tone of voice? Word choice? Timing?

POWER VERSES

Psalm 139:4; Psalm 37:30

An Unaccepting Heart

Wendy Pope

Blessed is the one whose sin
the LORD does not count against them
and in whose spirit is no deceit.

(PSALM 32:2)

I spent many years regretting sins from my past—sins that had hurt others and myself. Day after day, I replayed my decisions. Even decades later, the sting of past sins still had a hold on me.

I knew God had forgiven me; I'd asked Him to. So why couldn't I accept the freedom of His forgiveness? I wanted so badly to believe I was the person David describes in Psalm 32:2, yet it never happened.

Embracing the blessedness of forgiveness can be hard to do. It sounds all well and good, but too often the reality is that we are still carrying the weight of sin we can't seem to forget or forgive ourselves for. Yet, His Word assures us that God does not count our sin against us. So how can we live in this truth?

The first step is acknowledging our sins—to ourselves and to God. Confession *reconciles* our hearts with God's heart.

Then we begin to fill our hearts and minds with truth. Throughout the Bible, God teaches how an *unaccepting heart* can be changed and softened to accept His forgiveness. Consider these truths as a message for you from a loving God who longs to transform your life through the grace of His forgiveness:

My God doesn't condemn. "Therefore, there is now no condemnation for those who are in Christ Jesus" (Romans 8:1).

My master is grace, not sin. "For sin shall no longer be your master, because you are not under the law, but under grace" (Romans 6:14).

My Savior Jesus has set me free, therefore I am free. "So if the Son sets you free, you will be free indeed" (John 8:36).

My old is gone; because of Jesus Christ I am new. "Therefore, if anyone is in Christ, the new creation has come: The old has gone, the new is here!" (2 Corinthians 5:17).

Are you lugging a load of sin that God has already forgiven and for-gotten? Are you ready to stop living in shame, shackled by regret? Life is too short to exchange the freedom of grace for the bondage of our unbe-lief. Allow God to wash away the hurt and regret from past sins with the transforming power of His truth. Pray for an accepting heart that lives in the freedom of God's grace and forgiveness. That is a prayer God is sure to hear and answer.

Dear Lord, by faith I accept Your forgiveness and refuse to be a slave to forgiven sin any longer. I confess and move on! I commit to believing Your transforming truths and accept Your offer to live fully and freely in grace. In Jesus' name, Amen.

REMEMBER

You were not created to carry the weight of your sin. Jesus carried it for you, straight to the cross.

REFLECT

How will your life be different when truth takes root in your heart?

RESPOND

Help truth defeat the lies by writing the four truth statements from this devotion on an index card. Tuck them in your Bible or purse and read them aloud today.

POWER VERSES

Isaiah 1:18; Isaiah 43:25

When Your Husband Has Given Up

Lysa TerKeurst

For you formed my inward parts; you knitted me together in my mother's womb. I praise you, for I am fearfully and wonderfully made. Wonderful are your works; my soul knows it very well.

(PSALM 139:13–14 ESV)

The rejection. The harsh words. The absence of intimacy. The questions. The lack of answers.

My heart aches for anyone in a struggling marriage. I've been there. Many of us have. But I think the deepest hurt comes when one spouse gives up while the other is still trying. A panic arises to somehow make the other person wake up, get them to reengage, and help both of you fix this relationship.

A situation like this is much too complicated for simple answers. But might I give you one stepping-stone upon which to stand in order to stop the panic and balance yourself?

Decide today that you are worthy.

Because you are. Worthy. You may not feel like it. But a quick glimpse at Psalm 139 assures me, you are. And I'd rather depend on the solid truth of God than a roller coaster of fickle feelings.

You are beautiful and captivating and attractive and smart and capable. But if you are in a relationship full of unmet expectations, unresolved issues, and frustrating communication, I suspect you feel a little less than that.

Broken-down relationships can break down a woman. And if you're like me, when you feel broken down, those around you get your worst. Then, upon all the hurt and anxiety, you layer regret and shame. You start to feel like you've lost yourself—lost that girl inside you who used to be strong, happy, and ready to take on the world. The only way to recapture her is to come up for air and remember you are worthy. Then you can act worthy.

Step aside from the emotional yuck to make some levelheaded decisions. Get a plan. Talk to wise people who love you and will walk this tough journey with you. Draw some boundaries with your husband, if needed. Pray like crazy for clear discernment.

Remember, you can't control how he acts and reacts, but you can control how you act and react. Reclaim who you are.

I pray your relationship survives. I pray it with every fiber of my being. But if it doesn't, I pray most of all that the beautiful woman you are rises above all the yuck, still clinging tightly to the only opinion that matters — from the One who forever calls you worthy.

Dear Lord, my marriage is struggling. I'm struggling. Help me, please. I need to hold on to Your truths that I am worthy. And God, please show me what steps to take to support my marriage. In Jesus' name, Amen.

REMEMBER

You are worthy. God says so.

REFLECT

What has happened this week that makes you feel unworthy?

RESPOND

Memorize Psalm 139:14: "I praise you because I am fearfully and wonderfully made; your works are wonderful, I know that full well."

POWER VERSES

Isaiah 54:10; 2 Thessalonians 3:16

She Stands Alone

Glynnis Whitwer

Therefore, my dear brothers and sisters, stand firm.
Let nothing move you. Always give yourselves fully
to the work of the Lord, because you know that
your labor in the Lord is not in vain.
(1 CORINTHIANS 15:58)

Wiping beads of sweat from my forehead, I pushed the shopping cart toward my car, quickly unloaded my groceries, jumped into the car, and blasted the air conditioning in hopes of cool relief. After pulling onto a back-street shortcut toward home, I saw her.

She was a petite figure in a black dress standing on the sidewalk in front of a tall building. Though she faced the building, I could see she held a Bible. Her head was bowed over the cradled book as she stood in the sweltering heat. Alone.

It took just a moment to pass her, but her image stayed with me. It's not that I haven't seen people standing in front of buildings, but this wasn't a bank or a restaurant. There was no bus stop in front. The young women who routinely entered this building were broken, and they weren't going in for healing. And on that hot summer afternoon, one woman stood there praying for them.

She stood alone for what she believed God had asked her to do that day. In the heat. Enduring discomfort, odd looks, and probably some derisive comments. Some might say her sacrifice made no difference. We'll never know. We'll never know whose plans might have been changed by her steadfast obedience.

Moments before, I just wanted out of the heat. But her conviction challenged me to ask: *For what cause am I willing to stand alone?*

The sight of her touched me deeply because I know the exhaustion of battle fatigue. I've sat in frustration rather than standing firm. I know what weary feels like when it seems my efforts aren't making a difference.

Some days, I'm tired of standing for what I believe in. I think others would stand taller, or with less exhaustion. They'd deal with discouragement better than me. They'd show mercy where I show frustration. Maybe someone else could—maybe they *should*—take over for me.

That's when the image of this humble woman comes to mind. And the Lord says to me: *You just think she's standing alone. She's not. I'm right next to her. And I'll be right next to you. Keep standing.*

So I breathe in and breathe out. I picture the precious sister standing in front of the building. Only this time, she's not alone. In my mind I see Jesus standing beside her.

And on my own street, in my own life, in my own home, facing my own calling, wondering if I'm making any difference, I determine to stand another day. For a cause I believe in, for the cause of Christ, wherever He calls me to stand.

Dear Lord, thank You for reminding me that when I think I'm standing alone, I'm not. Thank You for being my hope in difficult times, and holding me up when I want to sit this one out. Help me to remember You are a very present help in times of trouble. In Jesus' name, Amen.

REMEMBER

We can stand firm for what we believe, knowing Jesus is always standing with us.

REFLECT

Are you facing a challenge that feels overwhelming? Imagine Jesus standing next to you. What kind of help would you ask from Him?

RESPOND

Write a letter of encouragement to someone who is standing for what they believe in. Let them know you respect and admire them for their steadfast faith.

POWER VERSES

Romans 14:7; Isaiah 41:10

Filling the Gaps

Lynn Cowell

*"I made you. I am now your husband. My name is The
LORD Who Rules Over All. I am the Holy One of Israel.
I have set you free. I am the God of the whole earth."*
(ISAIAH 54:5 NIrV)

I never thought I'd marry the guy I'd crushed on since sixth grade and whose name I'd doodled on my folders! Twenty-five years later, while far from perfect, there is one secret that's helped make our marriage strong. A secret I'm passing on to our daughters.

A man can never fill the love gap in your heart.

As women, we long for a love that will fill the hungry places in our hearts: to feel loved, cared for, pursued, desired. And while people can help fill those gaps, they can never fully satisfy our desires. Our hearts will always search for the only One who can truly give us the love we were created for.

The prophet Isaiah tells us who can fill our love gap: the Lord. Isaiah goes on to say we're set free from searching for love when we allow ourselves to be satisfied by God's love instead.

Yet, the cultural messages we are inundated with while growing up — from movies, songs, digital media, and books — try to convince us the perfect man is out there. Princess-like fantasies of being adored, affirmed, and attended to grow in our minds. *If only he would pay attention to me. If only he would say I am his, then I would really be happy.*

When I was growing up, a popular radio song promised that one guy would be my all-in-all: "I'm forever yours ... faithfully." But for some of us, the man we married has *not* stood by us faithfully. For others, there hasn't been a man who's said, "I do." Where does this leave us? Are we stuck feeling empty or broken for life?

I've walked beside several friends who've dreamed of picket fences, two kids, and a dog. Yet their dreams haven't come true. But while on a journey they never intended or would have chosen, they too have discovered the truth that no man can ever fill the love gap in their hearts.

No man but one … Love Himself.

Seeking Jesus has helped heal my loneliness and rejection and replace them with joy and acceptance. Looking to Him each day to meet my need for affirmation has taken the pressure off my husband.

I recently shared this truth with a friend as she wept, "If I had only known that my husband couldn't meet all of my needs! If I had only known that Jesus alone could fill me with the love I was missing … I wouldn't have divorced my husband last year."

Oh that we would grasp this truth and share it with the women in our lives. No matter what comes, we can find true love—a love that will never disappoint, never leave, never reject. It is a faithful love that can fill the gaps in our hearts.

Dear Lord, set me free to place my needs for affirmation, approval, and affection on anyone but You. I know You will never disappoint me, leave me, or reject me. In Jesus' name, Amen.

REMEMBER

No man can fill the love gap in your heart. No man but One, Jesus.

REFLECT

How do you look to others to fill the love gap in your heart?

RESPOND

Think of your favorite love song. Sing it today to your True Love.

POWER VERSES

Jeremiah 31:3; Song of Songs 2:16

Letting God Fill My Empty Places

Renee Swope

You God, are my God, earnestly I seek you;
I thirst for you, my whole being longs for you,
in a dry and parched land where there is no water.

(PSALM 63:1)

It was a source she'd come to depend on. A place she went to get her needs met. But it was never enough; every day she came back for more. Filling her jar with water, the woman looked up and heard Him ask her for a drink. Then He offered her something in return: *living water*. He said the water He offered would satisfy her so deeply she'd never thirst again.

"You have nothing to draw with and the well is deep. Where can you get this living water?" she asked (John 4:11).

She didn't realize Jesus wanted to satisfy a deeper thirst in her heart—a longing He Himself had created and one that only He could satisfy. All He needed to draw with was His Spirit. As far as the depth of the well, it was her heart He was looking into. She was the only one who could prevent Him from reaching the parts that needed Him most.

I know that place of needing Jesus to look into my heart and show me the emptiness only He can fill. Like the woman at the well, I've depended on other means to get my needs met. Yet, when I look to other sources instead of to Him, I always come up empty.

I've looked to people: family and friends, bosses and boyfriends, teachers and mentors. I've longed for their approval and the affirmation that comes with it.

I've also looked to possessions and positions and mistakenly put my hope in recognition. I've thought, *If only I had*, or *if only I could …*

But no matter how much I do or get, it's never enough to fill me up. And it's not supposed to. Because the empty places in our hearts were created to be filled by God alone. The deepest thirst of our souls can only be quenched by Him.

We see this deep thirst even in King David, who had everything: the highest position, unlimited possessions, and great power—yet none of it was enough. He described himself as parched and thirsty for God: "You, God, are my God, earnestly I seek you; I thirst for you, my whole being longs for you, in a dry and parched land where there is no water" (Psalm 63:1).

Then David described what he experienced when he drank deeply of God's love: "Because your love is better than life, my lips will glorify you. I will praise you as long as I live, and in your name I will lift up my hands" (Psalm 63:3–4). The same thing happened to the woman Jesus met at the well. She drank deeply of His love and was filled to overflowing.

God put a longing in our hearts intended to lead us back to Him. Only His unconditional acceptance, approval, and affirmation can fill the empty places in our hearts—the deepest thirst of our souls. Until God's love and acceptance are enough, nothing else will be.

Dear Lord, show me the empty places in my heart and how I can position my heart to be filled and fulfilled by the fullness of Your love. In Jesus' name, Amen.

REMEMBER

Jesus wants to satisfy a deep thirst in your heart—a longing He Himself has created and one that only He can satisfy.

REFLECT

How would your emotional state differ if you really believed and trusted that God fulfills?

RESPOND

Think back to ways Jesus has filled you in the past. Fill a pitcher with water. For every time you remember Jesus satisfying you, pour water from the pitcher into a cup. Keep filling until it overflows, knowing that is how Jesus longs to fill you.

POWER VERSES

Psalm 143:8; Jeremiah 2:13

How to Let Peace Rule

Samantha Evilsizer

Let the peace of Christ rule in your hearts.
(COLOSSIANS 3:15)

No more able are we to drive the rain back in the clouds by holding hands to the sky ...

Or stretch a rainbow's colors wide by scurrying to grasp its tail ...

Or force the tides to retreat by running at the sea ...

No more capable of these feats are we, than pursuing and capturing peace.

Peace.

That for which the world wars. Families crumble. People roam. That for which we compromise, improvise, and televise: *It's here ... if only you race after it with your time, your money, your life.*

But for all our chasing, we never lay hold of peace. Not until we reckon with the truth that there is only one true source of peace, and it is available free to all. The Bible says it in just nine words: "Let the peace of Christ rule in your hearts" (Colossians 3:15).

If we are to find peace, we must become students of the One who is our peace, Jesus Christ. He who is the Word. And this bit of Word, "Let the peace of Christ rule in your hearts," is a fine mentor.

This truth teaches us to slow down. Those two words—*let* and *rule*—intend to "umpire" our hurried hearts. So when circumstances crumble and we worriedly scramble to right them, we are taught to pause and call our hearts to peace. How do we do this? Through intimate knowledge of He who is our peace.

- Christ is trustworthy, as His resurrection proves. (Matthew 28:1–10)
- Christ controls the storms, as calmed winds and waves attest. (Mark 4:35–41)
- Christ knows every detail, as His healing power shows. (Mark 5:21–43)

It will take time to teach our hearts to let peace rule. Umpires don't begin careers in the World Series. Indeed, umpires go through rigorous training and schooling. They must work for years in the minor leagues before even dreaming of the majors.

We too must set our hearts and minds to learning and training. A good place to start is with the minors. Calling our hearts to peace when running late, when dinner burns, when scrapes and bruises happen, when fender benders occur. This is our practice and preparation for when the doctor calls, the pink slip arrives, the papers are served, and the accusations fly.

We call our hearts to trust in the One who is faithful to us in the small things, so that we learn His character again and again. This gives our hearts the training we need to know He is as trustworthy with the big things as He is with the in-between things. He is trustworthy with everything.

Dear Lord, You are my peace. Teach me Your ways; direct me in Your truth. Calm my hurried heart. I want to know You more and more. In Jesus' name, Amen.

REMEMBER

If we are to find peace, we must become students of the One who is our peace, Jesus Christ.

REFLECT

It will take time to teach your heart to let peace rule. To prepare you for the big things, what small things can you trust God for?

RESPOND

Memorize one of these verses about peace today. Call them out to your heart when trouble comes. "You will keep in perfect peace those whose minds are steadfast, because they trust in you" (Isaiah 26:3). "Peace I leave with you; my peace I give you. I do not give to you as the world gives. Do not let your hearts be troubled and do not be afraid" (John 14:27).

POWER VERSES

Isaiah 26:3; John 14:27

The Treasure of Thrown-Away Food

Lysa TerKeurst

Give thanks to the LORD,
for he is good;
his love endures forever.
(1 CHRONICLES 16:34)

If there was ever a secret for unleashing God's powerful peace, it's developing a heart of true thanksgiving. I came to understand this truth while reading a paper written by my son Jackson.

He wrote about the corruption and greed that caused the civil war in his native land. You see, for the first thirteen years of his life, Jackson lived in a forgotten orphanage in Liberia. As I read, I was impressed with the great job he had done recounting the facts of what had happened. But what made the facts so compelling was that Jackson wasn't just reciting the details of an historical event—he was recounting his experience of living through the horrific conditions of this war.

At one point, Jackson described what it felt like to be naked, digging through the trash for the treasure of thrown-away food.

The treasure of thrown-away food.

I can hardly type those words without crying. This is my son.

And yet, despite the horrific conditions of his childhood, there was an inexplicable thread of peace woven through his story. It was a powerful peace centered in the awareness of God's presence.

Truly thankful people are truly peaceful people. They have made it a habit to *notice*, *pause*, and *choose*. They *notice* everything they can be thankful for no matter what their circumstances. They *pause* to acknowledge each thing as a reminder of God's presence with them. They *choose* to focus on God's presence until His powerful peace is unleashed in their hearts.

How can we be noticers, pausers, and choosers? Women of thanksgiving no matter what circumstance we're facing?

I find this truth about the power of thanksgiving over and over in Scripture. What was the prayer Daniel prayed right before being thrown in the lions' den and witnessing God miraculously shutting the lions' mouths? Thanksgiving.

After three days in the belly of a fish, what was the cry of Jonah's heart right before he was finally delivered onto dry land? Thanksgiving.

How does the apostle Paul instruct us to pray when we feel anxious (Philippians 4:6)? With thanksgiving.

And what is the outcome of each of these situations in which thanksgiving is proclaimed? *Peace*. Powerful, inexplicable, uncontainable peace.

One of Webster's official definitions of *thanksgiving* is: "a public acknowledgment or celebration of divine goodness." I wonder how we might celebrate God's divine goodness today? I wonder what might happen if we decide in the midst of our circumstances today to notice, pause, and choose something for which we can truly be thankful.

Dear Lord, I ask You to help me notice things for which I can be thankful in each circumstance I face today. Please help me to pause and acknowledge each gift as evidence of Your presence. Help me to choose to focus on Your presence until Your powerful peace rushes into my heart and helps me see everything more clearly. Thank You for the reality that gratitude truly changes everything. In Jesus' name, Amen.

REMEMBER

Truly thankful people are truly peaceful people. They have made it a habit to *notice*, *pause*, and *choose*.

REFLECT

What do you notice around you in this moment that you are thankful for?

RESPOND

Commit today to keeping a thirty-day gratitude journal. Beginning today, list five things for which you are thankful.

POWER VERSES

1 Corinthians 15:57; 1 Chronicles 23:30

I Need Her

T. Suzanne Eller

"A new command I give you: Love one another.
As I have loved you, so you must love one another."
(JOHN 13:34)

The text message read: "I don't care how busy you are, Suzie. Put me on your calendar. You need me."

Sometimes friendship gets last place in my life. My parents need me more than they once did. I have children and grandchildren in three states. I juggle ministry, relationships, and the demands of real life.

But my friend is right. I need her.

When we get together over lunch, we laugh and catch up with each other's lives. Often, we find ourselves talking about God. We dig deep, asking questions, praying, and encouraging each other. And I love it.

So why do I let this really great friendship slide to last place?

In John 13, Jesus commands the disciples to love each other. Jesus didn't drop commandments lightly. He knew his followers needed each other. One day soon, He would return to heaven. Though His love would always be with them, His physical presence would not. And hard times were ahead.

Persecution. Suffering. Mistreatment.

But His command went even deeper than that. "As I have loved you, so you must love one another," He said (John 13:34).

What did that look like?

When Peter denied he ever knew Jesus, he stumbled from the scene weeping. Can you imagine how he felt? To love Peter "as Jesus did" meant that his friends couldn't give up on him. Instead, they would remind him of Jesus' love and forgiveness. They would point him toward redemption and grace.

We were never intended to live our faith in isolation. God and girlfriends are not just fun extras—they are required essentials. In good times. In hard times. When we are living with purpose. When we falter.

Perhaps you are thinking, *I don't have a friend who texts or calls me. I wish*

I had a friend like that. If so, pray and ask God for one person you know who needs someone and take the initiative to reach out to her. Sometimes we have to be the friend we wish we had by taking the first steps toward the friendship we need.

I am working on this gift called friendship. I've decided not to allow a week or a month to go by without a lunch date, or at least a conversation. In fact, I just texted my friend: "I don't care how busy I am, friend. Let's make a date. I need you."

Dear Lord, thank You for my friend. I get so busy that I sometimes put her last. Give me wisdom to know how to nurture this part of my life. Help me to love my friend the way You love me. In Jesus' name, Amen.

REMEMBER

We were not created to go it alone.

REFLECT

If your friend were to describe you, what words would she use?

RESPOND

Contact a friend today. Send a note of encouragement or call her to set up a time to get together.

POWER VERSES

Philippians 2:4; Romans 13:8

Define Yourself

Wendy Blight

For we are God's masterpiece.
He has created us anew in Christ Jesus,
so we can do the good things
he planned for us long ago.
(EPHESIANS 2:10 NLT)

"Define yourself through the hands and eyes of a true artist."

As I closed the stall door in a public restroom, that slogan caught my attention. It was the headline on an advertisement for a plastic surgeon. Reading those words, I knew this doctor was tapping into longings every woman has: to be beautiful, loved, and accepted by others.

But for most women, this is not reality. We don't see our beauty or worth. We look in the mirror and see only faults. We allow others to define us by what we're *not*.

Sometimes we get these messages from our culture. But other times they come from the people we love — parents, friends, our spouse. Their words deceive us into thinking we are unworthy and unlovely, failures as women and even as children of God.

Yet God created us to be women of strength and beauty, each of us with a divine purpose planned by Him before we were born. God alone has the right to define us. No one else.

There is only One true artist and His name is God.

God is *the* Creator.

The truth about our true identity isn't pasted on the back of a bathroom door; it's lovingly written across the pages of Scripture.

You are:

- Created in the image of God. (Genesis 1:27)
- Fearfully and wonderfully made. (Psalm 139:14)
- Precious and honored in His sight. (Isaiah 43:4)
- Redeemed and forgiven. (Ephesians 1:7)
- A new creature in Christ. (2 Corinthians 5:17)

- Holy and blameless before God. (Ephesians 1:4; 1 Corinthians 1:30)
- Chosen by God. (1 Peter 2:9)
- God's masterpiece. (Ephesians 2:10)
- Created with purpose to do great works for God's kingdom. (Ephesians 2:10)

You are God's creation—beautiful, strong, and created with a unique plan and purpose. Rest your head on your pillow tonight knowing and believing who you are *in* Christ. Pray for God to reveal to you who you really are—not who you are in the eyes of your parents, your spouse, your children, your friends, or even in the eyes of the world. May you know who you are in *your Father's eyes*.

> *Dear Lord, thank You that You are my Creator. Thank You that in You and You alone I find my identity. Father, open my eyes to see who I am in You. Make every truth I learned in this devotion a reality in my life. In Jesus' name, Amen.*

REMEMBER

You are God's creation, created in His image, beautiful, strong, and with a unique plan and purpose.

REFLECT

How do you see yourself? After reading this devotion, how do you feel God sees you?

RESPOND

The apostle Paul's second letter to the Corinthians teaches us that in Christ we are a new creation; the "old" has gone and the "new" has come (5:17). What do you need to give up from your old life so that you can embrace your new life?

POWER VERSES

2 Corinthians 5:17; 1 Peter 2:9

Interrupt Me

Luann Prater

"I was a stranger and you invited me in."
(MATTHEW 25:35)

After five years of living in our house, my husband agreed we needed curtains on the windows. Deciding on just the right ones, at just the right sale price, was a challenge. In the span of a week, I had shopped all over town, finally found something I liked that was affordable, installed all the hardware, and meticulously ironed every inch of the drapes before hanging them on the rods. Then I took them down and started over. The gals in the drapery department at the local department store knew me by name.

All of this happened the week before Thanksgiving. And exchanging curtains at the mall was the last thing I planned to be doing the Wednesday before Turkey Day. But there I was, paying for another set of drapes at the register.

And there she was, Vivian. She breathlessly approached the counter asking to use the phone. This young girl had been dropped off at the mall to go to work, only to discover she wasn't scheduled. She needed to call someone to pick her up.

That's when I felt a familiar knock on my heart. Actually, it was pounding. I knew it meant God had an interruption planned.

"Do you need a ride?" I asked.

All activity stopped. She looked at me quizzically. The cashier waited to see what would happen. Vivian cocked her head to the side in disbelief. "Uh, yes."

"I'm leaving; I'll take you," came out of my mouth.

May I just say that giving a ride to a stranger was not on my agenda. My to-do list was a mile long and there was nothing on it about offering a ride to someone I'd just met. However, the truths of Matthew 25 were resonating within me. I knew God had asked me to be on the lookout for strangers to invite in—into my home, into my church, and, so it appeared, into my daily routine.

During the drive to Vivian's house, she told me about her six siblings. Because of her mom's drug abuse, five were adopted out of the family

161

six years ago, leaving just her and her brother. No one wants to adopt thirteen- and fourteen-year-olds, she explained. She had subsequently made decisions that had taken her down some wrong roads. We talked about church and she said she'd gone a few times, but didn't attend now.

"Vivian, God put us together today," I said. "He has a plan for your life. You didn't expect to run into me and I didn't expect to run into you, yet here we are. Unusual, don't you think?"

"Yes," she said, "no one takes a chance on anyone. I couldn't believe you offered me a ride."

I asked about her past and her hopes for the future. In twenty minutes, we bonded.

"Are you working Sunday?" I asked.

"No, I'm off," she replied.

"I'll pick you up for church if you want to go with us." She said she thought that would be great!

I got out of the car and wrapped her in a hug. Then I prayed for her as we both stood amazed at how quickly we'd connected.

I'm thankful for interruptions. God wants to interrupt us for His purposes, inviting Him and others into our lives in unexpected ways.

Dear Lord, please open my heart, my eyes, and my routine to Your divine interruptions. May it be said of me, "She's a woman who invited God in." In Jesus' name, Amen.

REMEMBER

God wants to interrupt you for His purposes, inviting Him and others into your life in unexpected ways.

REFLECT

Have you felt that "knocking" on your heart? How do you respond to what the Holy Spirit is prompting you to do in that moment?

RESPOND

Ask the Lord for a greater awareness of His "knocking" and of others around you who need your help.

POWER VERSES

Proverbs 16:9; Matthew 25:35–40

When I Need to Trust Him

Nicki Koziarz

But I trust in you, LORD;
I say, "You are my God."

(PSALM 31:14)

It was news that made my heart ache like no other. Nothing would ever be the same. I climbed into my car, buckled my seat belt, and sped down a dark country road. The night sky was clear, but I could barely see through my tears.

I flipped off the radio and screamed at God, "Why?! Why did You allow this to happen?" Pressing my foot on the brake, I pulled over and parked on the side of the road. The air was cold, and the silence was eerie.

Do you trust Me? I sensed God whisper.

The question arose through layers of doubt and skepticism. Truth be told, I did not trust God. Oh, I trusted Him when things were good, when life was easy. But in the lowest moment of my life? I didn't really trust Him.

I wish I could tell you Jesus showed up in my car that night and I've never distrusted God since. But that isn't the truth. It would be years before I could say I trusted God again. And even today I still sometimes have trust issues with Him.

Why is trusting God so hard? Perhaps the obvious answer is: *We can't see Him.* Then there's the sensible rebuttal: *God's ways are not our ways.* Or the cliché answer: *He's mysterious.*

But I think that trusting God is so much more than just an intellectual position we accept.

Trusting God is a response: being able to take God's promises and directly apply them to our circumstances.

In my desperate situation that night, what I really wanted to say to God was "I need to trust You more than ever." But I couldn't believe the words, much less say them.

On days filled with uncertainty and fear, this practice of verbally

163

placing our trust in God can be powerful. Today, as I continue to learn how to trust God more, here are some things I'm saying aloud:

- Jesus, I need to trust You more than ever to believe that You work all things for my good. (Romans 8:28)
- Jesus, I need to trust You more than ever to fight this battle I am facing. (Exodus 14:14)
- Jesus, I need to trust You more than ever to be my God who provides beyond my limitations. (Philippians 4:19)

My inability to trust God that difficult night was largely a consequence of my own failure — I had fallen far from God. Yet in that painful moment, He was still the One I turned to. I can't help but believe it is in our moments of complete brokenness that we are most receptive to God's faithfulness and presence. These are the times we dare to turn to Him and learn to trust Him again.

Today, with what do you need to trust Jesus more than ever before?

Dear Lord, I am thankful for the trust You offer me. I ask today that You would help me to trust You more with every detail of my life. In Jesus' name, Amen.

REMEMBER

Trusting God is so much more than just a position we accept. Trusting God is a place of responding to His promises.

REFLECT

When was the last time you really trusted God for something? What was the outcome of those circumstances?

RESPOND

Write down on a card one of the "Jesus, I need to trust You" affirmations from this devotion. Keep it close by throughout the day and read it aloud each time you feel anxious about something.

POWER VERSES

Psalm 20:7; Psalm 140:6

The Need to Know

Lysa TerKeurst

*Then Peter said, "Silver or gold I do not have, but what I do have
I give you. In the name of Jesus Christ of Nazareth, walk."*
(ACTS 3:6)

I have a friend who is hurting. Life as she knew it has suddenly tipped over
into a raging river of chaos and confusion. She can barely come up for air
before another current rips her under. If ever there was a drowning with
no water involved, this is where my friend is.

Maybe you have a hurting friend too.

Yesterday, I sat down to write my friend a card and send her a little
gift. I wanted to love her through my words. My heart was full of care,
compassion, and a strong desire to encourage, but I struggled to translate
what I felt to paper.

As I prayed about it, the word *value* kept coming to mind.

*Remind her she is valuable. Remind her how much you respect her. Remind
her she is a woman who has so much to offer.*

In Acts 3, Peter and John encountered a crippled man at the temple
gate called Beautiful. They stopped. They noticed. They decided to touch.
Riches weren't available to them, but the ability to value was.

"Peter said, 'Silver or gold I do not have, but what I do have I give
you. In the name of Jesus Christ of Nazareth, walk.' Taking him by
the right hand, he helped him up" (Acts 3:6–7). The man in need was
worth touching. The man in need just needed someone to give him a
hand and help him up. After he got up, he went into the temple courts
praising God and stirring up wonder and amazement about what God
had done for him. The man who'd been in need became the man who
had so much to give.

I want my friend to know she too can get up. She too can stir up
amazement and wonder about our God.

Yes, she is valuable.

And so with imperfect words on a simple card, I wrote, "I just think you need to know you are so very valuable. I respect you and love you. Thank you for being you."

Who in your life might need a card like this from you today? Why not stop right now and write it before the moment slips away.

Dear Lord, thank You for reminding me how to love others. Help me to be Your hands and feet today. Give me Your heart so I can see who else in my path today needs some encouragement. For when I reach out, You reach in . . . into my heart and bless me so. In Jesus' name, Amen.

REMEMBER

We are all precious in God's sight. Someone in your life needs to hear that today.

REFLECT

What words of encouragement from friends have been meaningful to you in the past?

RESPOND

Write a note now to someone you think might need words of encouragement.

POWER VERSES

Psalm 94:19; 1 Thessalonians 5:11

Following My Husband's Lead

Renee Swope

However, each one of you also must love his wife as he loves himself,
and the wife must respect her husband.

(EPHESIANS 5:33)

I grew up in a family of multiple divorces and marriages led by strong women. When I got married, I had serious issues about respecting and following my husband's lead. Honestly, I was afraid if I submitted to my husband I'd become a doormat and lose myself in the process.

About a year after we got married, JJ told me it was easier to just let me lead because it wasn't worth the inevitable argument that followed if he tried. You'd think that's what I wanted—to get my way—but it wasn't. Instead of loving my husband more for giving me my way, when he became apathetic, I simply lost respect for him.

I knew our problem was mostly my fault. Deep down, JJ wanted to lead but when he tried, I often criticized *how* he led. I also knew Ephesians 5:33 commands wives to respect their husbands, but I wanted it to be more of a suggestion. It's not.

So, I started praying God would change JJ and make him easier for me to follow—that he'd be more decisive, more confident, and, well, just more of what I wanted him to be so I would *feel* respect for him.

One day, God strongly impressed on my heart that my control and criticism weren't getting me any closer to my desired outcome. In fact, my frustration with JJ only contributed to his doubts about his ability to follow God and lead our family.

God challenged me to keep my mouth closed when JJ did something I did not like or led in a way I didn't want to follow. Instead, I was to make every effort to encourage my husband's leadership by telling him things I admired and appreciated about him.

I started looking for and finding things in my husband I'd never noticed. I pointed out what I respected about him and let God take care of things I didn't. I made many choices to honor him in big and small ways. And do you know what? I discovered countless things about my husband that were worthy of respect.

I discovered that my fear of losing myself was unfair and unfounded. My husband didn't want me to become a doormat. He wanted my input, but he also needed my trust and encouragement. He needed me to believe in him and to offer my support—verbally, emotionally, and spiritually.

I've learned to follow my husband's leadership by trusting God's lead in JJ's decisions. Has it been easy? Nope. There have been job changes I didn't want him to make, financial investments that seemed too risky, and parenting issues that were hard, but my husband has become the leader of our family. And I've become more comfortable following his lead than I ever thought I'd be!

Dear Lord, I want to respect my husband. Help me to measure my thoughts and words carefully and come to You with my complaints. I want to become my husband's biggest cheerleader and watch You do Your work in his life. In Jesus' name, Amen.

REMEMBER

Wives are called to respect their husbands.

REFLECT

How do you express value and respect for your husband? Do you tend to spend more time criticizing or encouraging him?

RESPOND

Within the next twenty-four hours, tell your husband at least one thing you are thankful for about his character, his work ethic, his provision, his humor, or something he adds to your life.

POWER VERSES

1 Peter 3:15; Proverbs 17:9

God Never Wastes Our Pain

Glynnis Whitwer

But he said to me, "My grace is sufficient for you, for my power is made perfect in weakness." Therefore I will boast all the more gladly about my weaknesses, so that Christ's power may rest on me.

(2 CORINTHIANS 12:9)

She'd betrayed me again. Hurt and anger simmered as I walked away counting to ten, then twenty. I felt ashamed as I thought about my heart's reaction toward my child. *Shouldn't I be above this? Shouldn't I be able to deal with rejection and deceit without getting angry?*

That day, as always, God let me vent. As I presented my raw emotions to Him, He poured peace over my heart, sustaining me for another day.

It's been seven years since God added to our family through an international adoption. We didn't know the trauma our girls had experienced, but God did. And although some adoption stories have fairy-tale endings, ours has been punctuated by nightmares as our daughters' suffering has become ours.

In the years since the adoption, I've learned a lot about living with pain and helplessness. I've also had to decide what I believe about God's character. Mostly I've had to dig deep into whether or not I believe God can truly bring good out of all pain, or if my daughters' suffering and ours is just a waste.

What I've come to believe is that God will never waste my pain, but I can. When I'm not honest about the reality of how hard life is, I waste God's offer of peace. When I try to do things in my own strength, I waste God's offer of power. When I keep the pain to myself and pretend everything is perfect, I waste opportunities to minister to others walking a similar path.

But when I confess my feelings of inadequacies, when I admit I'm helpless to heal the wounded ones in my care, I move into a place of reliance—and that's just where God wants me. For in this place of dependence, God takes center stage. Although I'd remove the pain and trauma

169

with a snap of my fingers if I could, I know God is working even in this —*especially* in this.

I understand better now how the apostle Paul could be glad for his weakness. I'm not glad for sin or what caused the brokenness we face. But I see the pain for what it is—a condition of this fallen world and a place for God's power to work. This perspective helps me face another day. My circumstances haven't changed, but hope has seeped in through the cracks.

No pain is wasted when I submit myself to God's plans. And even now, we are seeing God's healing power in the lives of our two precious girls.

Dear Lord, we've been here before, with me asking for relief. Help me to accept my weakness in this situation and to allow Your power to take over. I admit I don't understand how this works, but I'm choosing to trust Your Word. In Jesus' name, Amen.

REMEMBER

God will never waste your pain, but you can.

REFLECT

Think about a painful time in your life. How was God's power revealed during that time?

RESPOND

It's easy to allow painful circumstances to bring us to a place of bitterness. If you are in that place today, write down ten things you are thankful for.

POWER VERSES

1 Corinthians 1:25; 1 Peter 2:20

More than Crumbs

Tracie Miles

"Give us today our daily bread."
(MATTHEW 6:11)

As I sat on the beach enjoying the sunrise, I watched a few seagulls wander aimlessly, looking lost and confused. I wondered why there were so few in a place where there are normally multiple flocks that swarm overhead filling the air with screeching cries.

Then I realized they had no reason to be on the beach, much less to be excited or active. There were no people around to generate crumbs.

I'm pretty sure seagulls can smell potato chip crumbs a mile away. They stay at a distance until they think someone has something they want. Then they come running, or should I say dive bombing. Even if no birds are in sight, one tiny crumb falls on the sand and suddenly dozens of seagulls swoop down out of nowhere.

Memories of hungry seagulls interrupting our picnics at the beach made me chuckle until I felt God whisper to my spirit: *Sometimes, Tracie, you are just like those seagulls.*

In Matthew 6, Jesus teaches His disciples how to pray, in what is commonly referred to as the Lord's Prayer. This devotion's key verse is taken from the middle of the Lord's Prayer. In it, Jesus reminds His disciples to stay in close union with Him through prayer, because He knows they need the spiritual nourishment and physical necessities only He can provide. Jesus calls His disciples to seek Him and trust His provision for their daily needs.

Unfortunately, there are times I don't follow this wisdom and instruction. I may go days or weeks, aimlessly wandering like those seagulls on a deserted beach—flying through my tasks and routines, without consciously seeking God.

But as soon as something happens that makes me mad, sad, worried, frustrated, discouraged, or stressed, I fly straight to God. Swooping in out of nowhere, I dive-bomb into His presence. Expectantly, I wait for Him

171

to give me a profound thought or an answer to prayer. In essence, to toss me some crumbs of spiritual encouragement.

Unlike a seagull who seeks temporary satisfaction from random crumbs, I want to be consumed with a spiritual hunger that's never satisfied. A hunger that pains me if I fail to get a daily portion of God's wisdom, love, and guidance. A hunger that, when met, replaces my discouragement, worry, and stress.

I don't want to live with a seagull mentality, being satisfied with mere crumbs. Instead, I want to enjoy the fullness of God's presence and a constant supply of His Word each and every day. What about you?

Dear Lord, forgive me for not seeking You daily. I ask for Your physical provision and spiritual nourishment to get me through every day. Help me to develop an insatiable desire for Your Word and to spend time with You in prayer. In Jesus' name, Amen.

REMEMBER

God's Word sustains you and keeps you spiritually nourished so you will have the trusting faith and spiritual energy to handle life's adversities.

REFLECT

In what ways do you tend to have a "seagull mentality"?

RESPOND

Make a commitment to set your alarm clock thirty minutes earlier tomorrow, and begin forming a habit of spending time in God's Word every morning.

POWER VERSES

Matthew 6:26; Psalm 73:26

A Call and Response

Samantha Evilsizer

Some trust in chariots and some in horses,
but we trust in the name of the LORD our God.

(PSALM 20:7)

His wee body curls in the crook of my arm. So tiny, so new, only two days old. Six pounds and fifteen ounces, yet he bears the name of a weighty truth. Timeless and eternal.

"His first name is Zachary," his parents tell me. "It means 'remembered by Yahweh.'" Anytime God reminds us in His Word that He remembers, it's an affirmation of His faithfulness, that we're always on the Lord's mind.

"His middle name is Kael. It means 'faithful,'" they said. "Put together, his two names are a call and response."

This newborn's first name calls to mind the richness of God's character: unfailing and sure. Every time he says his name, he'll recall the Lord's goodness. His middle name elicits a response: *Yes, Lord. Because You are faithful, so shall I be.*

God is ever calling, desiring our minds, hearts, and wills to respond to who He is. His names testify to every attribute He possesses.

I'm intrigued by all this naming, so I open the Word to know more about the name I call upon.

- *El Shaddai* means God Almighty. He is the only God who is omnipotent, omnipresent, omniscient—the only one who knows our needs and who completely nourishes, satisfies, and supplies as a mother would her child. He is our sustainer. (Genesis 17:1; 28:3; 35:11; 43:14; 48:3)
- *El Roi* is the God who sees. Not one of our pains or needs is beyond His sight. (Genesis 16:13)
- *Jehovah Nissi* means the Lord is my banner. In battle, nations flew their banners at the front lines. This gave soldiers hope and a place to focus. God gives us encouragement and a focal point in the midst of our battles. (Exodus 17:15)

173

- *Jehovah Rapha* is the God who heals. Our Great Physician restores us and heals our physical and emotional wounds. (Exodus 15:26)
- *Jehovah Mekoddishkem* is the Lord who sanctifies you. God calls us to holiness and gently reminds us that it is He Himself who sets us apart for His sacred purposes. (Exodus 31:13; Leviticus 20:8)

To know God's names enables us to respond when He calls. He calls to our minds and our thoughts respond. He calls to our hearts and our emotions respond. He calls to our wills and our actions respond.

El Shaddai calls: *I satisfy.* We respond: *I will be nourished by You.*

El Roi calls: *I see you.* We respond: *I will find comfort in You.*

Jehovah Nissi calls: *I cover you.* We respond: *I trust Your protection.*

Jehovah Rapha calls: *I heal.* We respond: *I open my heart for You to heal.*

Jehovah Mekoddishkem calls: *I make all things new.* We respond: *I believe You create beautiful things from dust.*

There are many names of God throughout Scripture that help us become better acquainted with the Lord. So when troubles call, we respond by putting our faith in Him. With every birth, death, and life lived in between, we call on the One who is faithful.

Dear Lord, You are worthy of a mind that meditates on You daily, a heart that loves You steadfastly, and a will that follows Yours. When You call, help me respond according to who You are: faithful. In Jesus' name, Amen.

REMEMBER

God is ever calling, desiring your mind, heart, and will to respond to who He is. His names testify to every attribute He possesses.

REFLECT

What name of God from this devotion most resonates with your present circumstances?

RESPOND

Select one name of God from this devotion. Decide today how you will respond in faithfulness to God based on the name you choose.

POWER VERSES

Nehemiah 9:5; Jeremiah 9:24

Affair Proof Your Mind

Lysa TerKeurst

"Watch and pray so that you will not fall into temptation.
The spirit is willing, but the flesh is weak."
(MATTHEW 26:41)

A few years ago, I watched as a friend got tangled up in an emotional affair. She was a strong Christian woman who loved her family, but her attraction to this other man seemed unavoidable. She tried to talk herself out of it, but her heart played tricks on her mind and the justifications for letting things go just a little further soon led her to a very dangerous place. She had become emotionally attached to him.

In a moment of desperation and fear, she confided in me about what was going on. As she described how she got pulled into this place, I was challenged by how subtly it happened. She'd always prided herself on being a woman of strong conviction and had scoffed at the idea of ever being tempted to have an affair.

It starts off simply—a comment made that you mull over one too many times; a conversation in which you feel a surprising connection; a glance that lingers just a second too long; or one of a thousand other interactions that seem innocent yet aren't.

We must never assume it couldn't happen to us. We are all just a few poor choices away from doing things we never thought we would.

And the time to prevent an emotional affair is before it ever starts.

Jesus warned His disciples, "Watch and pray so that you will not fall into temptation. The spirit is willing, but the flesh is weak" (Matthew 26:41).

Watch. I need to be aware that I am just as prone to temptation as anyone. One of the best ways to be watchful is to pray *with* and *for* my husband. We need to be open and honest about meeting each other's needs and investing wisely in our marriage.

Be sensitive to the subtleties. When another man says or does something I wish my husband would say or do but doesn't, it can diminish the esteem I have for my husband and build up this other man. This is a seed of poison.

175

Be spiritually equipped. I must park my mind on the truth, and the truth is I am married to an amazing man. He is not perfect and sometimes our marriage can be hard, but I made a commitment to him in a covenant before God and there are no biblical reasons in our marriage why we should ever part.

My friend did the hardest but wisest thing she could in telling me about her emotional affair. It helped her to see she needed to flee and have someone else hold her accountable. But it also helped me. Her admission made me aware and alert to dangers lurking in any kind of unhealthy emotional connection with another man.

Dear Lord, may I forever treasure my marriage and consider it worthy of protection. Help me to be a courageous woman who flees from any and every situation where there is even a hint of danger. In Jesus' name, Amen.

REMEMBER

The time to prevent an emotional affair is before it ever starts.

REFLECT

What specific things do you need to flee in order to protect your marriage? Delete your Facebook or Twitter accounts? Change your phone number or email address? Go to a different coffee shop or gym?

RESPOND

Are you struggling in this area? Confide in a friend or mentor to help hold you accountable. If you know of a friend who is struggling, call her to meet up so you can encourage her face-to-face.

POWER VERSES

Proverbs 14:1; John 8:11

What's Your Message?

Lynn Cowell

*Only be careful, and watch yourselves closely so that you do not forget
the things your eyes have seen or let them fade from your heart as long as
you live. Teach them to your children and to their children after them.*

(DEUTERONOMY 4:9)

My heart breaks when I see my girls struggle. It's hard to watch them navigate the treacherous waters of high school relationships, especially when waves of rejection slam against their hearts. I often feel like I'm in the storm with them. Why do I feel vulnerable when I see the tears in their eyes?

Perhaps it's because memories of my own turbulent teen years are not too far removed. It's all too easy to recall the confusion, pain, and slights of that era in my life. However, along with the difficult memories, I am also aware of deep gratitude for those growing years. I'm so thankful God sent amazing friends into my life when I was a young woman. I'll never forget the ones who helped me discover that no man could fill the love gap in my heart. Only Jesus could fill what He created.

I am also thankful God placed me in my daughters' lives to share this truth with them. You see, when Jesus showed me He was the only One who could satisfy the emptiness of my heart, He didn't just give that truth for me. Jesus offered me His truth so I could pass on His radical love to my kids — and perhaps even my grandkids one day. Deuteronomy 4:9 affirms that we have opportunity and influence in the lives of our children and others.

What is one truth God has revealed that you can pass on to your children, your children's children, or young people in your world? Are there revelations or treasures from His Word, glimpses into His heart that He's given to you? If so, they are not just for your benefit, but also for your family and those in your sphere of influence.

Has the Lord given you a clear understanding of forgiveness? Teach your child the process of working through a grudge. Have you experienced the Lord's healing? Come alongside those in your life as they mend.

Do you cling to hope because God has lifted your spirits? Share that with another who's in the middle of grim circumstances.

Don't take for granted all the Lord has done in your life. Instead, take the message He's given you and share it with others, intentionally passing on the truth and stories of God's faithfulness for generations to come.

Dear Lord, help me to be intentional in sharing the truth You have revealed to me. Help me to make the most of the message You've given me by passing that truth to the next generation. In Jesus' name, Amen.

REMEMBER

God has taught you His truth not just for your benefit, but also for your family and those in your sphere of influence.

REFLECT

What two or three truths has the Lord made real to you through the experiences of your life?

RESPOND

Briefly identify the times and situations in which your child is most open to spiritual conversations. Use the next opportunity to share with your child one of the truths the Lord has made real in your life.

POWER VERSES

Deuteronomy 6:6–9; Ephesians 6:4

I Can't Think Straight!

Glynnis Whitwer

If any of you lacks wisdom, you should ask God,
who gives generously to all without finding fault,
and it will be given to you.

(JAMES 1:5)

I felt like I was walking in circles. My to-do list was long and I had accomplished nothing on it. Why couldn't I think straight!? Urgency pulled and anxiety tugged, yet I couldn't seem to make a wise decision about what to do next.

Have you ever felt like that? Some days I just plod along, hoping beyond hope that somehow I'll pull myself together. Sadly, my success rate those days is low. Trying to do more is pointless when my mind is scattered. And that seems to be my biggest challenge these days — a cluttered mind.

For years, I never thought to ask God for help to think straight and make decisions. Maybe I'd bring Him in on the big decisions, but the little ones I figured I could handle myself. Then I read this passage with new eyes:

> If any of you lacks wisdom, you should ask God, who gives generously to all without finding fault, and it will be given to you. But when you ask, you must believe and not doubt, because the one who doubts is like a wave of the sea, blown and tossed by the wind. That person should not expect to receive anything from the Lord. Such a person is double-minded and unstable in all they do (James 1:5–8).

I'd been trying for years to manage on my own. And when I did ask for help, doubt hindered my ability to hear God's answer. I needed to change my expectations about God, and then invite Him into my daily decisions.

Once I started asking God to clear my mind and direct my decision making, I had to trust He was doing just that. After praying, if I sensed I was supposed to do a specific task, I did it, trusting that God was giving me wisdom. The more I trusted that nudge, the more I experienced God's leading.

Listening and trusting are important parts of prayer, because the purpose of prayer is not always getting God to move. Many times, prayer positions us to hear God's direction on how *we* should move. Through prayer, we align our hearts to God's heart, and things become clearer.

Is the clutter in your mind making it difficult to think clearly? Are you trying to figure things out on your own? We've been given the mind of Christ and we are offered the wisdom of God. Ask and receive.

Lord, You know how hard it is for me to focus sometimes. It's hard to figure out what needs to be done. I just feel overwhelmed and discouraged. I know You aren't a God of confusion, so I ask for Your wisdom and clarity to help bring order to my chaotic thinking. In Jesus' name, Amen.

REMEMBER

God longs to bring clarity, focus, and wisdom to your thinking if only you'll ask for His help and believe He will answer.

REFLECT

Are there areas of your life that seem harder than others to figure out? Why do you think that is?

RESPOND

If you feel overwhelmed, sit down and ask God to show you His priorities for you. Write down what He tells you, and thank Him for His faithfulness.

POWER VERSES

Romans 8:6; Isaiah 26:3

Swim Lessons

T. Suzanne Eller

But when he saw the strong wind and the waves,
he was terrified and began to sink.
"Save me, Lord!" he shouted.
(MATTHEW 14:30 NLT)

When I was a little girl, my father decided it was time for me to learn how to swim. He took me by an arm and leg, swung me high, and tossed me into the lake. I landed in the water with a splash, popping my small head up like a turtle, coughing and sputtering. Somehow, I dog-paddled to shore.

This was how my dad's father had taught him to swim, and so he thought it was the best way to teach me. Personally, I believe a pair of floaties would have been helpful.

Perhaps Peter felt the same way in Matthew 14. The waves from an impending storm were already rocking the disciples' boat when Peter suddenly saw someone walking toward them on the water. The other men were terrified, but Peter leaned in closer.

It was Jesus!

"Don't be afraid," Jesus called out.

"If it's You, tell me to come to You," Peter replied.

"Come," Jesus said.

Peter leapt out of the boat. But within seconds, reality hit. Peter couldn't walk on water, much less swim in the cascading waves. In terror, he cried out, "Save me!" Jesus reached out His hand and caught him, and together they made their way to safety.

We tend to focus on Peter's fear when we read this story, but what about his faith? Peter wasn't certain of his own abilities. He wasn't sure how to overcome the waves. He simply jumped into the water because Jesus bid him come.

There are times in my own life when I have heard my Savior invite me to step out of the boat: *Trust Me in this. Don't look at the waves; look at Me. I'm not going to let you sink.* But I am afraid. I am aware of my limitations.

181

I see the challenges, and I experience the obstacles once I'm in the water. Yet, I also know that the outcome isn't dependent on my ability, but on my obedience to His call.

The difference between my earthly father—whom I love in spite of the fact that he threw me into a lake without benefit of floaties—and my heavenly Daddy, is that I am never left to dog-paddle alone to shore. Jesus is right there with me. To teach me. To help me through the rougher waves. To remind me of Who to trust when I feel ill equipped.

Perhaps you feel Jesus calling you to a swim lesson—to go deeper in your relationships, in your faith, in ministry—and discover a new level of trust as you leap out of the boat.

So take the risk—jump!

Jesus is there, His arms open wide. He's your Savior, and He knows exactly what you can do with a swim lesson or two.

Lord, I feel You calling me to deeper waters. I've held back out of fear. Help me to take my eyes off the obstacles and place my focus on You. Thank You for lessons that allow me to reach for Your strong arms and trust in Your plan. In Jesus' name, Amen.

REMEMBER

Success isn't always about how fast you reach the shore; it's trusting that in the midst of the waves He'll help you find the way.

REFLECT

What is one swim lesson Jesus is teaching you right now? How are you responding?

RESPOND

Put your toes in the water. Write down one realistic small step that you can take today to go deeper in your relationships, in your faith, or in ministry.

POWER VERSES

Isaiah 41:13; Isaiah 43:2

But I Really Don't Like Her

Samantha Evilsizer

Do nothing out of selfish ambition or vain conceit.
Rather, in humility value others above yourselves.
(PHILIPPIANS 2:3)

The showdown had begun. She at one end of the table, me at the other. My plate a smoking gun; lima beans my bullets.

I wish I could say I was a two-year-old, throwing a tantrum. Instead, I'm embarrassed to admit I was twenty-five, sticking it to a woman I couldn't stand. Meeting her stealthy gaze, I methodically slid one lima bean after another to the side of my plate. I wouldn't take one bite of her potpie until it was clear of them.

It's not that I disliked lima beans. What I didn't like was my boyfriend's mother. My own mother's voice grew loud in my head: *It doesn't matter what she's done; eat the limas, Sam. Put down your disdain and put her above yourself.*

With determined purpose, I jabbed the last lima. Without a word, I said it all to her: *I will not honor your meal. I will not honor you.* My mom's voice grew still louder in my head: *Use humility, Samantha Elaine!*

After dishes were washed and guns put away, another voice resonated. The Lord spoke gently, yet firmly. *I've asked you to not be selfish. This was a perfect opportunity to show humility. She took time to cook that meal; you should have put her above your desires and eaten* all *of it.*

I was ready with my rebuttal. *But I really don't like her! She's controlling. She doesn't respect me or my relationship with her son. She's impossible to get along with, much less honor.*

As far as I was concerned, she was the enemy and my duty was to draw battle lines. Yet, deep down I knew my actions shouldn't be determined by hers. After all, she'd worked hard on that dinner. She was my boyfriend's mom. And most importantly, she was my sister in Christ.

God called me to be humble. I knew He was inviting me to honor her, not only by eating her meal, but by also complimenting her special dish. It would've been a small thing, a God thing—but I didn't do it.

Although that relationship—with the boyfriend and his mom—has ended, my relationship with humility has grown. And continues to grow as I challenge myself. It may be something as small as eating food I don't care for, watching a movie that bores me, attending a function I'd rather not. Or maybe speaking kind words when frustrated, praying for someone who's offended me, or taking a back seat when I want to be in front.

By being humble, I honor God. There's joy in giving glory to the One who humbly laid down His life to give me eternal life. This truth provides me the grace I need to tuck my guns away and ask, "May I please have seconds?"

Lord, thank You for being the best example of humility and honor. Please give me the grace to respect others, especially those I find hard to respect. In Jesus' name, Amen.

REMEMBER

Even though it may be incredibly difficult, honoring others is always the better way to go.

REFLECT

What is your first reaction when you feel confronted? Ask a friend or family member if you're not sure. How can you process your reactions in light of the truths you learned in this devotion?

RESPOND

Who in your life right now is your equivalent of the boyfriend's mom? What is one thing you can do to "tuck your guns away" in humility and show kindness?

POWER VERSES

Romans 12:10; Colossians 3:12–13

Why I Want to Be More Leaky

Lysa TerKeurst

*As the rain and the snow come down from heaven, and do not
return to it without watering the earth and making it bud and flourish,
so that it yields seed for the sower and bread for the eater . . .*

(ISAIAH 55:10)

On my back deck are two identical flowerpots. They were planted at the same time. They contain the same flowers and soil. They both get the same amount of water, shade, and sun. They're similar in every way, but they look vastly different.

One is thriving. The other is not.

One is full of lush cascading blooms and is an absolute delight to look at. The other has a few gangly sprigs of color among brownish leaves, not exactly a gardener's pride and joy.

I asked my husband why he thought the two containers were so different. "Simple," he said. "One's got holes so excess water can leak out and the other doesn't."

Interesting.

The one that has the ability to leak out excess water is thriving. The one keeping all the water in its container is not such a beautiful display.

This morning I was reading Isaiah and it made me think of my flowerpot situation:

> As the rain and the snow come down from heaven, and do not return to it without watering the earth and making it bud and flourish, so that it yields seed for the sower and bread for the eater, so is my word that goes out from my mouth: It will not return to me empty, but will accomplish what I desire and achieve the purpose for which I sent it. You will go out in joy and be led forth in peace; the mountains and hills will burst into song before you, and all the trees of the field will clap their hands. Instead of the thorn bush will grow the juniper, and instead of briers the myrtle will grow (Isaiah 55:10–13).

Water is supposed to be poured in, nourish growth, and then leak out so it can evaporate, having accomplished what it was created to do. It was never supposed to be poured in, sit stagnant, and be hoarded by the container, thus stunting the growth of life within.

So it is with God's Word.

God's Word should be poured into our lives, nourish growth, and leak out through the way we live. People should notice we've spent time in God's Word. They should see our joy and peace.

We should be a little less prickly than the thorn bush and briers. We should be a little more lovely like the juniper and myrtle. We should leak God's Word.

Which got me thinking about how I respond to criticism. It's not enough for me to just respond properly when I am criticized. I should use those criticisms to remind me how much the world is desperate for encouragement. I should be leaky with positive emails or thank yous to the businesses and ministries and staff members of my church who bless me week after week.

I'm not one to criticize. But I also shouldn't be one to stay stagnant either. In order to be the grand display of God I want to be, I need to be more holy … or holey, as the case may be.

The one who leaks is the one who thrives.

Lord, forgive me for being stagnant. I want Your Word to leak out of me so others see peace and joy. In Jesus' name, Amen.

REMEMBER

God's Word should be poured into our lives, nourish growth, and leak out through the way we live.

REFLECT

Are you more likely to respond to criticism with grace or harshness? Are you more critical than encouraging?

RESPOND

Who have you criticized recently? Be "leaky" today by writing an encouraging email, calling to say thanks, or sending a note of kindness.

POWER VERSES

Psalm 42:1; Psalm 63:1

Unexpected Grace

Tracie Miles

God's law was given so that all people
could see how sinful they were.
But as people sinned more and more,
God's wonderful grace became more abundant.

(ROMANS 5:20 NLT)

He appeared out of nowhere. The dreaded blue lights flashed on as soon as I passed his unmarked SUV. I instinctively checked the speedometer. Sure enough, I was speeding. My stomach knotted as I prepared to receive the penalty for exceeding the speed limit.

My fingers tapped in irritation on the steering wheel, and my scowl deepened as the police officer walked to my window.

"Ma'am, I stopped you for speeding. Driver's license and registration, please."

Then it happened. The unexpected. The unwarranted. The undeserved. The policeman glanced into my car and checked out my passengers — three kids and a husband. Then he startled all of us by blurting out a big ol' "Hey!" to my husband, calling him by name. Apparently, they grew up together, and they proceeded to spend a few friendly minutes getting reacquainted. The officer handed back my license and registration and gave me a smile.

"Slow it down please, and have a good day."

Stunned by the unexpected mercy, we breathed a collective sigh of relief as I drove away — slowly. I hadn't paid attention to the law. My guilt was undeniable and I had no excuse. I deserved to suffer the consequences, but instead I was given grace.

Grace is undeserved favor or pardon. We can't earn it or buy it. It's something the giver bestows out of the goodness of his or her heart. The Bible tells countless stories of people who received grace, including prostitutes, unfaithful marriage partners, liars, and more. Their sins deserved punishment, but when they asked God for forgiveness, His grace wiped their guilt away. They were treated as pardoned offenders, just as I was.

The apostle Paul reminds us that, despite our sins, God is good and gives grace in abundance (Romans 5:20). The more we need, the more we get.

Although God hates sin because it separates us from Him and ushers pain into our lives, His grace is available no matter how big our offense. We receive grace, forgiveness, and mercy when we accept the pardon that was purchased through the sacrifice of His Son.

As much as I appreciated the officer's grace, it paled in comparison to God's grace. The officer's grace was one of kindness but not one of redemptive love. It was a grace of compassion but not the lifesaving grace Jesus gives.

The truth is, I deserved a speeding ticket, but grace was given. In the same way, we deserve punishment for sin, but God's forgiveness and favor are offered anyway ... through the gift of His unwarranted and undeserved grace.

Dear Lord, thank You for undeserved grace. Forgive my sins and shower me with Your favor, even though it is undeserved. Thank You for loving me enough to grant me pardon. In Jesus' name, Amen.

REMEMBER

Jesus died for our sins and He keeps no record of wrongs. Even when we deserve punishment for our choices, His grace and love are unconditional.

REFLECT

Consider how God's grace is undeserved, yet He gives it anyway. Is there someone to whom you need to offer grace?

RESPOND

Spend time thanking God for His gift of unending grace. Write instances of His grace to you on small slips of paper. Put them in a jar and keep adding to them each day. Let this overflowing visual reminder be an encouragement for you to share abundant grace with others.

POWER VERSES

Acts 15:11; Romans 3:23

Finish What You Start

Glynnis Whitwer

" 'My food,' said Jesus, 'is to do the will of him
who sent me and to finish his work.' "
(JOHN 4:34)

I excel at starting projects. Especially those that include a trip to the office supply store, where I can stock up on new notebooks, file folders, and pens. Optimism abounds at the beginning of something new.

Then reality hits. What initially seemed fun quickly becomes hard work. Discouragement sets in. Perfectionist tendencies stifle my ability to move forward and it begins to seem easier to give up rather than finish what I started.

Part of my challenge is lack of focus. There's so much I want to do that my thoughts are often scattered. I allow myself to be pulled in multiple directions, intrigued by the possibilities of a new and exciting project. Plus, sometimes I do things just because I can. This approach frequently leaves me with a to-do list that's seriously undoable.

Finishing well requires discipline that doesn't come naturally. But it's key to living a manageable life that reflects God's priorities for me. So while my shelves include books on time management and productivity, the best role model of finishing well is Jesus.

Jesus is the picture of focus and discipline, especially in the midst of many people demanding His attention. In the book of John we read a story about Jesus sitting by a well while His disciples went for food. As He waited, a solitary woman came to draw water and Jesus engaged her in a life-changing conversation—not only for her but for her entire village.

On this day, Jesus could have pleaded exhaustion or frustration. He'd been traveling, it was warm, and He was hungry. Just one of those challenges would have been enough to derail me. Instead, Jesus narrowed His focus to one woman and finished the assignment God gave Him for her.

After His disciples returned, they tried to get Jesus to eat. He responded: "My food ... is to do the will of him who sent me and to finish his work" (John 4:34). Jesus knew what His Father had asked

189

Him to do and was committed to do it. He models clarity of purpose, perseverance, and compassion — all characteristics I want.

If you feel like you are always starting things and never finishing, perhaps it would help to focus on only one or two things God is calling you to today. Don't try to tackle everything at once. Ask God for His priorities and concentrate on doing your best in those areas.

Changing lifelong patterns of not finishing things takes time. I've learned that when I submit my overwhelmed feelings to God, He gives me strength to persevere.

Dear Lord, thank You for forgiving me when I fall short. Help me to be like Jesus, focused on Your will and work. Show me Your priorities for my life. In Jesus' name, Amen.

REMEMBER

Finishing well requires discipline.

REFLECT

Is there something you know God wants you to do, but you haven't done it? What is it?

RESPOND

Identify one or two areas you believe God wants you to focus on. Ask God to help you align all areas of your life with His priorities for you.

POWER VERSES

Hebrews 10:35 – 36; James 1:2 – 4

When Doubt Won't Go Away

Renee Swope

*"Pardon me, my lord," Gideon replied, "but how can I save Israel?
My clan is the weakest in Manasseh, and I am the least in my family."*

(JUDGES 6:15)

A few years ago, I was struggling with paralyzing self-doubt. I'd made a ministry commitment to do something big, something I'd never done before. Although I had initially felt assured God was calling me to this, now that I was in the middle of it, I wasn't so sure.

For days, I pleaded with God, asking Him to zap me with confidence and take away all my doubt, but He didn't. Instead, He led me to the story of Gideon, a man who was called by God yet paralyzed by feelings of inadequacy. From reading his story in Judges 6, I knew Gideon overcame his doubts and fears by focusing on what God thought about him instead of what he thought about himself.

The first thing he did was speak honestly with God about his bout with doubt. When the angel of the Lord told Gideon to go defeat the Midianites, Gideon protested, "How can I save Israel? My clan is the weakest ... and I am the least in my family" (Judges 6:15).

Recent conflicts and defeats had shaped Gideon's perception of himself and caused him to question his ability to fulfill God's calling. The same was true for me. A conflict with a friend that week made me question whether or not I should even be in ministry. *If I couldn't maintain healthy relationships at all times in all areas, how could I help others?*

I also received negative feedback on a project that week. One harsh criticism overshadowed several positive comments and consumed my focus.

When conflict arises at work or at home, do you ever feel like these challenges disqualify you from other ministries or callings? Does criticism ever paralyze you or keep you from believing you can do certain things?

God used Gideon's story to show me that overcoming doubt is about changing the way I think, which changes the way I feel, and can eventually transform the way I live.

The next time you start feeling insecure, ask God to show you what triggered your doubt. Then process the trigger point through God's perspective. Search His Word and ask Him for His wisdom. Then choose to focus on His thoughts toward you instead of your thoughts about yourself. For instance …

When doubt says you can't do something because it's too hard, remember God says you can do all things through Christ who strengthens you (Philippians 4:13). Or when doubt tells you that you will never figure things out, remember God says to trust Him with all your heart and lean not on your own understanding; to acknowledge Him in all your ways, and He will make your paths straight (Proverbs 3:5–6).

Without a doubt, God wants you to live with a confident heart. Some days it will be about what He's calling you to do, but even more than that, it will be about what He wants to do *in you* as you learn to completely depend on Him.

> *Lord, I'm tired of my bout with doubt. Show me what triggers my*
> *insecurity and help me to rely on Your thoughts about me instead*
> *of my thoughts about myself. I want to learn how to live in the security*
> *of Your promises. In Jesus' name, Amen.*

REMEMBER

Every doubt we have can be replaced by a truth in God's Word.

REFLECT

How do conflict and criticism affect your confidence?

RESPOND

What triggers your doubt and insecurity? Process the trigger point through God's perspective by replacing that misgiving with a Scripture. Focus on His thoughts toward you instead of your thoughts about yourself.

POWER VERSES

Jeremiah 17:7; Luke 1:45

A Hopeful Future

Samantha Evilsizer

Then Job replied to the LORD:
"I know that you can do all things;
no purpose of yours can be thwarted . . .
My ears had heard of you but now my eyes have seen you."

(JOB 42:1–2, 5)

This past year, people I love had to grapple with some very difficult things — home foreclosures, loss of businesses, suicide attempts, drug overdoses, deaths of loved ones, extramarital affairs, children imprisoned, another year of unemployment. In the midst of such hardships, it's easy to doubt that God can redeem the pain, recover what's lost, heal all that's broken. Can He truly fit the pieces of the past into a hopeful future?

If I look only at my circumstances and rely on what my circumstances imply, I'm apt to believe the Lord isn't able. However, circumstances can change, and unless I'm anchored to something unchanging, my faith will rise and fall with my circumstances.

God never changes. His power to give a hopeful future never changes. His Word never changes. So when life weaves threads of doubt into my mind about God's authority, I reread accounts of His faithfulness and redemption throughout the Bible.

While Job's family, home, and health were being demolished, God was preparing to give him double of what had been killed, stolen, and damaged.

While Joseph was a slave and prisoner, God was planning for him to be second in command over Egypt.

When Ruth was a homeless, barren widow, God was creating a home for her with Boaz. She would become a wife, mother, and great–great-great-grandmother to Jesus.

The moment David laid down in adultery with Bathsheba, God was laying the groundwork for him to rise up in repentance.

As Moses killed an Egyptian with his hands, God saw him chiseling the Ten Commandments with those same hands.

When Peter lost faith and denied Christ, God knew Peter would soon boldly proclaim Christ to thousands.

While Mary watched Jesus dying on the cross, God saw Jesus resurrected and seated on His heavenly throne!

No matter how dire the circumstances, God turned each story into a hopeful future. None of God's plans can be thwarted. God can reverse, restore, revive, and renew. He sees beyond our present troubles and sparks a fire to light up the future with hope.

Be on the lookout for His plans. Trust Him. He can take any circumstance and use it for your good and His glory.

Dear Lord, thank You for Your faithfulness. And for recording stories of dreary pasts turned into hopeful futures. Please do the same for my circumstances. In Jesus' name, Amen.

REMEMBER

No matter how bleak your situation, God can use it for your good and His glory.

REFLECT

Who do you know whose circumstances are dismal? How are you seeing God turn them around? In what ways does that encourage you for your own situation?

RESPOND

God never changes. His power to give a hopeful future never changes. His Word never changes. So when life weaves threads of doubt into your mind about God's authority, reread accounts of His faithfulness and redemption throughout the Bible.

POWER VERSES
Genesis 50:19–20; Psalm 40:5

Mistaken Identity

Karen Ehman

"Whoever belongs to God hears what God says."
(JOHN 8:47)

I poured a cup of coffee and logged on to my laptop to peek at a friend's Facebook page. When I tried hopping over to see her latest pictures, I couldn't get her name to appear in the search bar. I was puzzled. This had always worked before. Glancing at the top of the screen, I realized I wasn't logged in to my own account. My son had forgotten to sign off when he'd been on earlier so I was actually logged in as him instead.

I couldn't get where I wanted to go because I had mistaken my identity.

With a quick click of a mouse, I switched accounts and used Facebook as "me." Operating under the right identity, I was free to view pages, leave comments, and get where I wanted to go.

Sometimes in life we encounter the same issue — we don't realize we're operating under a mistaken identity. We log in to our day and encounter wrong thinking that makes us forget who we really are. This may happen when a voice from the past or our own negative self-talk urges us to forget our identity in Christ. We're blocked by doubt and can't get where God is calling us to go — to a life lived with our security and value rooted deep in His thoughts toward us.

Instead we hear: *You can't do that. You aren't good enough. You'll never change. Why can't you be more like your sister? If only you were more* _____ *instead of so* _____ .

When statements of self-doubt claim our identity and discouragement sets in, we need to log out of the lies and log in to God's truth. It's the only way we will discover and live into our true identity in Christ — and the only way to navigate our lives according to God's Word.

Here are some truths I tell myself to remember my true identity: *I am the daughter of the Most High God. I am loved, redeemed, and renewed. I am chosen, blameless, and holy. I was bought at a great price. God knows me thoroughly and yet loves me completely. He has plans for my future that include hope, not harm; blessings, not banishment. I belong to Him.*

Jesus said, "Whoever belongs to God hears what God says" (John 8:47). We need to listen to God's Word, let it take root in our minds, and allow it to eradicate any untrue, destructive thought patterns. Replacing the negative chatter with assuring Scriptures will gently but firmly remind us who we are as children of God.

Yes, if we belong to God we will hear what He says. As we log in to His truths daily, we will no longer mistake our true identity. We will know the confident reality of who we are in Christ.

Dear Lord, when I am tempted to think of myself in a way that is neither healthy nor true, remind me both of who I am and to Whom I belong. In Jesus' name, Amen.

REMEMBER

Remember who you are in Christ in order to avoid assuming a mistaken identity.

REFLECT

What are some of the circumstances in which you typically find yourself doubting your true identity?

RESPOND

Make a list of Scripture phrases you can find of who we are in Christ. (Examples: chosen, holy, dearly loved, etc.) Whenever you are tempted to believe the opposite of any of these (I am rejected, unloved, etc.), repeat to yourself—out loud if you must—what God really thinks of you.

POWER VERSES

Romans 1:6; 1 John 3:1

Mean Girls

Lynn Cowell

But now you must also rid yourselves of all such things as these:
anger, rage, malice, slander, and filthy language from your lips.
(COLOSSIANS 3:8)

Standing in line for the concert gave my family plenty of people-watching time. As people made their way to the back of the line, I commented on all the immodest clothing. "Why would she wear those in public?" "Oh my! I can't believe she feels comfortable dressed like that!"

I must have shared quite a few of these statements because my oldest teenage daughter finally said, "Mom, you are being mean!"

I felt so small. I hadn't thought I was being *mean*. I was simply pointing out to my girls how *not* to dress. But my daughter was right.

The truth is, my girls already know how not to dress; I have been teaching them since they were five. And now I was teaching them how to judge other women. I was teaching them to be mean.

Since that night at the concert, I've come to the conclusion that mean girls often come from mean mamas. When we point out the flaws of others, we are modeling a judgmental heart. Instead, what we mamas need to demonstrate is compassion.

Scripture says we are to *rid* ourselves of slander, which means scandalous remarks (Colossians 3:8). The Bible makes no exceptions—there is never an occasion when it is okay to slander others.

One way we are overcoming mean-spiritedness in our family is through accountability. When my girls are gossiping or putting another girl down, I gently point it out—and my girls do the same for me. Having my child call me out was uncomfortable at first. But making this a family issue, rather than just me correcting my kids, is bringing us to a deeper level of kindness.

Like me, you may be surprised to discover just how often you say unkind things. If you watch each other's words, both you and your child will become more compassionate, less judgmental, and a whole lot more careful with what you say. It's working for me, and I trust it will work for you too.

Dear Lord, I want to rid myself of slander and in turn teach my children to do the same. Please cleanse my heart of judgment and help me to set a guard over my mouth. In Jesus' name, Amen.

REMEMBER

There is never an occasion when it is okay to slander others; the Bible makes no exceptions.

REFLECT

When do you find yourself most caught up in slander? With a close friend? In a certain environment?

RESPOND

Once you have defined the situation that tempts you to put down another person, plan right now how to avoid it.

POWER VERSES

James 4:11; Ecclesiastes 10:12

Three Marriage Lies

Lysa TerKeurst

[Love] always protects, always trusts, always hopes,
always perseveres. Love never fails.
(1 CORINTHIANS 13:7 – 8)

I know the heart-ripping hopelessness of a relationship unraveling. The coexisting. The silent tension. The tears. The early years of my marriage were very hard. We were two sinners coming together with loads of baggage, unrealistic expectations, and extremely strong wills.

There was yelling, door slamming, bitterness, and a desire to call it quits. There was this sinking feeling that things would never get better. That's when I first started hearing three lies: (1) I married the wrong person; (2) he should make me feel loved; and (3) there is someone else better out there.

As I began to believe these lies, a tangled web of confusion formed in my heart.

When I shared my frustrations about the whole situation with my friends, many nodded their heads in agreement, helping me to feel justified. But one didn't. She said, "I know what *you* think. But what does the Bible say?"

The Bible? I didn't think her religious question would help me. But over the next couple of days, I kept hearing her words.

With reluctance and skepticism, one afternoon I turned to a couple of verses she suggested, including 1 Corinthians 13. As I read the list of everything love is supposed to be, I felt discouraged. Our love didn't feel kind, patient, or persevering. The love in my marriage felt broken.

A few days later, I heard an interview on a Christian radio station in which a couple was talking about these same verses. Everything they said made me want to gag and change the station. *What do they know about how hard love can be?* That's when they said something that grabbed me: "Love isn't a feeling, it's a decision."

Wow.

I went home and flipped to 1 Corinthians 13 again. This time, instead of reading it like a list of how love should make me feel, I read it as if I could decide to make my love fit these qualities. *My love will be kind. My love will be patient. My love will persevere.* Not because I feel it—but because I choose it.

At the same time, God was working on my husband's heart as well. We decided to make some 1 Corinthians 13 love decisions. Slowly, the stone wall between us started coming down.

It wasn't easy. It wasn't overnight. But our attitudes and actions toward one another began to change. And I stopped believing the marriage lies. Eventually, I replaced them with three marriage truths: (1) having a good marriage is more about *being* the right partner than *having* the right partner; (2) love is a decision; and (3) the grass isn't greener on the other side; it's greener where you water and fertilize it.

Maybe you've believed the marriage lies too. My heart aches for you if you are in a hard place in your marriage. I know tough relationships are stinkin' complicated and way beyond what a simple devotion can possibly untangle. But maybe one of these three marriage truths can help loosen one knot ... or at least breathe a little hope into your life today.

Dear Lord, thank You for these truths, no matter how hard they are to read. Thanks for Your Holy Spirit, who gives me strength to turn from the lies and walk in Your truth. In Jesus' name, Amen.

REMEMBER

Having a good marriage is more about *being* the right partner than *having* the right partner. Love is a decision. The grass is greener where you water and fertilize it.

REFLECT

In what ways have you pulled away from your husband because of feelings of rejection, anger, or bitterness?

RESPOND

Share this devotion with your husband today. Let him know gently that you love him and that you want your marriage to thrive. Ask to pray together for wisdom on the next step to take.

POWER VERSES

1 Corinthians 13:4–8; Song of Songs 8:7

Your Thoughts Have Wheels

Tracie Miles

For as he thinketh in his heart, so is he.
(PROVERBS 23:7 KJV)

The day started fine but ended with confusion. As a timid middle-schooler, I climbed the steps of my school bus eager to get home. Sitting quietly in my seat, all of a sudden I got this sinking feeling. Although my surroundings appeared the same, something was not right.

The bus was the normal sunshine yellow, littered with the usual misplaced pencils and wadded-up papers, but I felt out of place. That's when I realized I did not know the kids around me. And I had never seen the bus driver. Frantically, I searched for anything familiar. My heart raced with panic as I realized, *I'm on the wrong bus!*

Although I was headed somewhere, it was not where I wanted to go. I'd been so distracted by thoughts of sleepovers and how much homework I had that I was not focused on where I was going. As a result, I ended up somewhere I did not want to be (though I finally did make it home!).

Thinking back on that day, I've considered how our thoughts determine a lot about the direction of our lives. Like the school bus, our thoughts will always take us somewhere, but it may not be where we really want to go.

If we spend time thinking about how the boss does not appreciate us, our thoughts will take us to a bad attitude at work.

If we focus on how much we do for others and how little we feel appreciated, our thoughts will take us to a place of resentment.

If we fume over something our husband or kids did, and mentally practice the harsh words we plan to say, those thoughts will lead us to arguments, hurt feelings, and damaged relationships.

If we dwell on why God has allowed problems in our lives, we will transport ourselves into insecurity and unhappiness.

If we focus our thoughts on money, career, success, and pleasure, we will find ourselves frustrated and discontent.

Our thoughts are powerful and require great self-control. If we allow them to run rampant, focusing on things that lead us away from God, we will wind up at a destination we would never deliberately choose. Scripture teaches us to carefully choose what we think about because our thoughts determine who we are and how we live.

My childhood memory reminds me to consistently keep my mind on God and the thoughts He has for me. That way I can live according to His plans and with His perspective, seeking to be aware of where my thoughts may lead me.

Our thoughts really do have wheels. Where are your thoughts taking you today?

> *Dear Lord, please help me to take my thoughts captive, focusing on things that are pleasing to You. Please give me the desire to honor You and abide by Your Word in any area of my thoughts I am struggling to do so. In Jesus' name, Amen.*

REMEMBER

Our thoughts are powerful and require great self-control.

REFLECT

What negative thought patterns can you identify?

RESPOND

Draw a picture of a road that forks. On one side of the fork, write down your negative thoughts and notice the destination to which they lead. On the other side of the fork, write down what God's Word says and determine to stay focused on His truth instead.

POWER VERSES

Philippians 4:8; Romans 12:2

God Is Working on Your Behalf

Samantha Evilsizer

Since ancient times no one has heard, no ear has perceived, no eye has seen any God besides you, who acts on behalf of those who wait for him.

(ISAIAH 64:4)

An ultimatum from my boss forced me into unemployment. She asked me to lead an initiative that went against God's Word. Fears clamored. I had no husband, no savings, no additional source of provision. I pleaded with God to intervene, to change my boss's mind. But it didn't happen. She made her decision, which solidified mine: I quit.

My mind raced: would I be able to pay rent, find a new job, hold onto hope? My financial, spiritual, and emotional accounts were depleted, and I couldn't see beyond my dreary situation.

God nudged me to send my resume to a ministry I knew rarely hired. I doubted they'd accept my application, and pushed aside the thought to apply. If only I'd lifted my eyes away from the unbelief, I might've realized God was working on my behalf, much like He did for Naomi.

You see, at the same time soil churned, seeds nestled underground, and crops waved in the wind, Naomi needed God to intervene. She lamented to her widowed daughter-in-law Ruth: "Even if I thought there was still hope for me—even if I had a husband tonight and then gave birth to sons—would you wait until they grew up?" (Ruth 1:12–13). Destitution — real and perceived—left her desperate. Can you feel it in this widow's words?

It would take time for Naomi to look beyond her dire circumstances and see divine intervention. God's redemption involved Ruth, the very person Naomi tried to dissuade from following her. Yet she was so engulfed by her emotions and circumstances, Naomi couldn't fathom how God would provide. "Call me not Naomi [pleasant]; call me Mara [bitter], for the Almighty has dealt very bitterly with me" (Ruth 1:20 AMP).

Perhaps your situation is bitter. You can't see how God is working. You don't have the energy to apply for one more job, so you turn down that lead. Your marriage is on the verge of collapse anyhow, so you cancel your counseling appointment. Life is bleak, so you withdraw rather than join friends for dinner.

If you are destitute financially, emotionally, spiritually, don't miss this: "So Naomi returned from Moab accompanied by Ruth the Moabite, her daughter-in-law, arriving in Bethlehem as the barley harvest was beginning" (Ruth 1:22).

Naomi's journey was hard and long. Yet she had to take a first step. When she arrived at her place of redemption, the harvest was beginning —a harvest that was gleaned by Ruth, the very person she'd pushed away. In that field, Ruth caught Boaz's attention. He ultimately provided for Ruth and Naomi for the rest of their lives.

Well before I turned in my two-week notice, the Lord tilled the heart of the director at that ministry I had initially disregarded. The director had created a new position and I was hired to fill it. Looking back, I wish I'd looked first for God's faithfulness instead of torturing myself with worry.

Though unseen, God is divinely intervening. If you're walking through a desperate place, look to the Lord instead of your circumstances. He's working on your behalf.

Dear Lord, I give up fear, doubt, and unbelief for hope, trust, and joy as I focus on You, not my circumstances. Thank You for working on my behalf. In Jesus' name, Amen.

REMEMBER

Even in the most desperate places, God is there, working on your behalf.

REFLECT

What specific aspects of Naomi and Ruth's story comfort you? How can you put the hope from how God rescued them into practice in your life today?

RESPOND

Fill in the blanks: Today I will trust and believe God for _____, because He is _____ and _____.

POWER VERSES

Psalm 66:5; Isaiah 25:9

An Overloaded Life

Glynnis Whitwer

Be sure you know the condition of your flocks,
give careful attention to your herds.

(PROVERBS 27:23)

We crammed suitcases, backpacks, and tote bags on a luggage cart and raced to the ticket counter, desperately trying to keep our three little boys in forward motion and the bags from slipping. My husband was pushing, and I was pulling, both of us trying to balance the overloaded cart. We were managing it all until we approached the elevator.

Seven-year-old Joshua ran ahead and held open the door with his body. But as we traversed the curb, bags started to fall. In the mayhem, we ran over three-year-old Robbie's foot. Robbie screamed, my husband yelled for help, and an alarm blared in the elevator because of the open door, causing Josh to cry. Within seconds, we were in a total meltdown. Somehow, we made it to our flight, but regrets hung heavy.

I wish that morning were an exception. Sadly, during that season of life, I always tried to finish one last task before leaving the house, fit one more errand into a busy afternoon, or take on one more thing than I could handle.

The problem? I had an overloaded life.

My responsibilities outweighed my capacity to manage them. Every day was filled with frustration and everyone in my family suffered. I needed God's help in a big way.

God gave me guidance from the Bible's book of wisdom: "Know the condition of your flocks, give careful attention to your herds" (Proverbs 27:23). That verse highlighted my problem area; I wasn't managing my responsibilities well. In fact, I wasn't even sure what my responsibilities were.

So I decided to begin listing everything on a notepad. I wrote down things I needed to do for home, work, and family. I listed small things, like phone calls, as well as big projects. It took days, and when the list was complete I wanted to burn it—it was that overwhelming.

Instead, I started to edit. After prayerfully seeking God's will, I crossed out responsibilities I no longer felt called to carry. I delegated things other people could do. I was able to edit some commitments immediately; others needed to be fulfilled before I could remove them from my schedule. Eventually, I whittled down my list to a manageable amount.

God has since added two girls to our family through adoption, so now I'm the mother of five. And I still tend to believe I can do more than I actually can. But I've realized my overly optimistic outlook can hurt me and my loved ones if I don't balance it with wisdom and careful consideration of the realities of my life.

I've learned the hard way that an overloaded life leads to meltdowns. But a well-managed life leads to balance and peace.

Dear Lord, You know how crazy and out of control my life can be. But You've called me to a well-managed life. Help me manage better what I can control, and release what I can't. I need Your wisdom and discernment today. In Jesus' name, Amen.

REMEMBER

An overloaded life will always lead to chaos, but a well-managed life leads to peace.

REFLECT

Overcommitment is often a sign of an unmet longing in our hearts. What hunger in your heart leads you to take on more than you should?

RESPOND

Write down everything you need to do over the next week or month. What changes can you make so you have more balance and peace?

POWER VERSES

Luke 12:42–43; Proverbs 31:15

Choice Points

T. Suzanne Eller

And your ears shall hear a word behind you, saying, "This is the way, walk in it," when you turn to the right or when you turn to the left.
(ISAIAH 30:21 ESV)

If the findings of a recent research study are true, I made at least five thousand decisions today. Seriously? Well, let's consider this ... I made a decision to get out of bed. I made a choice to put on my tennis shoes and run at 6:00 a.m. I chose peanut butter Cheerios® over oatmeal. I decided which bills to pay. What to make for dinner. Whether or not to answer a phone call. Which clothes to wear. Whether the plants needed watering or if they could wait another day.

Okay, I may indeed have made more than five thousand decisions today!

Some of our everyday choices are random, others weighty, but many of our decisions are choice points. Choice points are seemingly insignificant decisions, yet they lead us in one significant direction or another. For example, I choose whether to react in anger or respond with understanding to my husband. I choose whether or not to create drama with a friend who hurt my feelings. I choose time with my heavenly Father or push that time to another day ... again. I choose whether or not to say those words that cause my child pain.

Recently, I was on a mission trip and the team was exhausted after six days of demanding travel. We had missed a train and stood on the platform awaiting the next one. It was nearing midnight, cold, and wet. Our next scheduled event was early in the morning.

The coordinator walked over to me. "I'm so sorry," she said. "I didn't mean for it to work out this way."

There I stood at a choice point. I could share my frustration. I could explain that my sleep tank was on empty. I could say nothing, while sighing with a martyred expression.

As she waited for my reply, I reminded myself what a privilege it was to be there. That ease and comfort were never offered our Savior, and losing a little sleep was nothing compared to anything He went through. Everyone around me was just as tired as I was.

"I'm fine," I said. "In fact, it's been an amazing day and I can't wait to see what God does tomorrow."

She pulled me into a huge hug. "Thank you, Suz."

I wish I could say I handle every choice point that way. Sometimes I fail. But I'm praying I'll remember how much my choice points matter. You see, they don't just affect me; they affect those within the vicinity of my decisions, throwing them into a choice point of their own.

In the five thousand decisions you make today, how many of them will be choice points?

Dear Lord, I sometimes feel overwhelmed by all my choices, and it makes me cranky. Today as I make my five thousand decisions, walk with me, remind me of how my choices affect others, and help me to choose wisely. In Jesus' name, Amen.

REMEMBER

Your choice points don't just affect you; they throw others into choice points of their own.

REFLECT

Think back over the last week. What choices have you made in your difficult moments?

RESPOND

Wait to respond to a situation when you feel more poised. Whether a minute, an hour, a day, or a week, it will be based on thinking rather than emotions.

POWER VERSES

Proverbs 16:9; Psalm 25:9

When Worry Makes Me Weary

Renee Swope

"Come to me, all you who are weary and burdened,
and I will give you rest."
(MATTHEW 11:28)

As we drove home from a weekend in the mountains, I felt a heavy sense of dread. Laying my head back, I told my husband, JJ, "I don't want to go home." The stress and strain of countless commitments at home and work were taking a toll on me. I just wanted to head back to the mountains where I could rest.

JJ encouraged me to make a list of all my commitments and ask God what to cut back on. I took his suggestion, but much to my surprise, the changes I sensed God leading me to make weren't in my schedule — *they were in me.*

God didn't show me I needed to cut back at work or in ministry. He didn't reveal that our kids were in too many activities. He didn't lead me to take a sabbatical, although I was hoping He would. Instead, I sensed it was worry, not my workload, that was making me weary.

In the months leading up to this point, I'd spent almost as much time thinking and worrying about deadlines as I did working to meet them. Some days my concerns about commitments and meeting expectations consumed me. I was preoccupied with the possible outcome of several different decisions — simultaneously — and it left me depleted mentally, emotionally, and physically. But until I stopped and talked to God about it, I had not recognized my mental mayhem as worry.

My mind is wired to think a lot, so I'm used to the constant flurry of motion in my brain. Yet anxiety had slowly crept in, causing tangles in my thoughts, a tightening in my chest, and tension in my neck.

Instead of going back to the mountains to rest, I sensed God wanted me to find a resting place in His presence right in the middle of life. He invited me to come to Him with the worries that were making me weary.

Do you sense Him inviting you to come to Him today? He promises a place to quiet your thoughts in His presence. "Whoever dwells in the shelter of the Most High will rest in the shadow of the Almighty" (Psalm 91:1).

He offers freedom from the captivity of your concerns: "Then you will call on me and come and pray to me, and I will listen to you. You will seek me and find me when you seek me with all your heart . . . And [I] will bring you back from captivity" (Jeremiah 29:12–14).

Instead of letting your worries make you weary, respond to God's invitation and come to Him—asking, seeking, and finding a resting place for your restless thoughts.

Dear Lord, when my concerns consume me, help me remember to come to You. Show me if my workload or worries are making me weary and help me to trust You with both. In Jesus' name, Amen.

REMEMBER

God promises a place in His presence to quiet your thoughts.

REFLECT

When and where do you make time for a quiet place of rest? Have you said to the Lord, "I will come to You, for I am weary and burdened, and I know You will give me rest"?

RESPOND

Make a list of all your commitments and ask God what to cut back on. Are what consumes you external things, or internal things—worry, doubt, fear, stress?

POWER VERSES

1 Peter 5:7; Hebrews 4:16

Another Chance

Samantha Evilsizer

My beloved spoke and said to me, "Arise, my darling, my beautiful one, come with me. See! The winter is past; the rains are over and gone."
(SONG OF SONGS 2:10–11)

"I'll never know how much it cost to see my sin upon the cross."*

These lyrics caught in my throat the first time I sang them several years ago. I cried the ugly cry as I stared at my circumstances, ashamed. I'd made significant compromises in some areas of my life. Until the warm truth of that song caught me off guard, I had turned a cold shoulder to forgiveness. Shame had convinced me I wasn't worthy of another chance.

Last summer, I met a young woman who needed a second or third chance. On a 75 degree, gorgeous-in-every-way Los Angeles day, I served meals on Skid Row. There I was, navigating my way around hypodermic needles and people in pain. There she was, fidgeting outside the women's shelter.

Her demeanor matched the tattered gray condition of her sweatpants. Washed out and muted; buried under the debris of a dark world; away from the light for far too long. Inching toward me, she stepped over others hibernating beneath cardboard and despair.

Try as I might, I couldn't catch her eye as she asked for help. Shame from past deeds had beaten her down. It made her doubt she was worthy of anything, much less another chance for a hot meal and cold drink. This sweet woman had been pushed out of the food line. Unable to defend herself and in too much physical pain to stand in line again, she needed someone to make a way.

Together, we walked to the front of the food truck (not gonna lie, it was fun breezing past her bullies). But I felt ridiculous handing her scrambled eggs and water. Surely, she needed so much more.

We all do at some point, don't we?

She needed to know this place didn't have to be her last stop. That

---

*"Light of the World (Here I Am to Worship)" by Tim Hughes. © 2000 Thankyou Music.

what she'd done could be forgiven—forgotten, even. That this dark season could turn into a season of light. I wanted to share this truth: "See! The winter is past; the rains are over and gone" (Song of Songs 2:11).

Winter, that gloomy season, that *should* pass. But what if it lingers? What if one bad-for-us choice turns into a hundred that beat us to our own Skid Row? What if mistakes convince us we don't deserve another shot?

Been there? Me too. But letting in the light of Christ melts our winter of doubt into a spring of hope. What we've done doesn't dictate who we are. The truth is, what *He's* done makes us who we are: forgiven, hopeful, and worthy of another chance. We may not feel we deserve a second shot. But Christ's sacrifice and our salvation through Him gives us one.

Never doubt; He'll always lead us past the bully of shame to the front of the line for so much more than eggs and water.

Dear Lord, it's hard to believe I'm worthy of another chance. But I'm choosing to accept that Your death means new life for me. In Jesus' name, Amen.

REMEMBER

What we've done doesn't dictate who we are. The truth is, what He's done makes us who we are: forgiven, hopeful, and worthy of another chance.

REFLECT

Why is it sometimes difficult for you to believe you're worthy of another chance?

RESPOND

Write down every reason you feel you're not worthy of Christ's love and forgiveness. Now, read them out loud and say after them, "But Christ died on the cross to forgive me once and for all for that. I've repented and I'm forgiven."

POWER VERSES

Isaiah 12:1–2; John 3:17–18

Jesus Loves Those
in Messy Marriages

Lysa TerKeurst

"But blessed is the man who trusts me,
GOD, the woman who sticks with GOD."
(JEREMIAH 17:7 MSG)

I threw the cup of orange juice across the kitchen. It felt good to do something, anything, to release this surging anger. And I didn't even mind cleaning the pulpy, sticky residue. It felt soothing to know how to clean something. I knew how to wipe away this mess. And I liked seeing the mess disappear.

If only my marriage mess could be fixed with soap and water. If only. I whispered, *God, why does this have to be so hard?*

Many have been there. Whether in a really tough marriage or just in a rough patch, marriage can be messy. Hurtful. Lonely. No one ever told me about this side of marriage before I donned the white dress and danced to MC Hammer at the reception. But after twenty years of learning and pressing through the messes to see something beautiful form in the midst of it all, here's what I know: *Jesus loves those in messy marriages.*

He loves me and my husband in the midst of it all. Jesus doesn't love the mess of hurt, isolation, and bitterness. Those are things He wants us to work on. But He never stops loving us.

Yes. Jesus loves me. And His grace is strong enough to extend His love into every part of me. The good parts. The broken parts. The bitter parts. The loving parts. And even the part of me that throws orange juice.

Yes, He loves me.

And Jesus loves my husband. His grace is strong enough to extend His love into every part of him. The good parts. The broken parts. The bitter parts. The loving parts. And even the part of him that looks at me like I'm crazy when I throw orange juice.

Since Jesus loves both of us, He's the best source of help for our marriage. I don't say that without a deep awareness of how stinkin' hard it is

213

to go to Jesus when I'm mad as fire at my husband. And I certainly don't say it in naive simplicity. Gracious, you may be facing a marriage situation that rips your heart into a thousand pieces every day.

But still, I know Jesus is the best source of help. Honest cries for help lifted up to Jesus will not go unheard. He sees. He knows. He loves. And Jesus will direct you as long as you stick with Him. Consider these words from Scripture: "But blessed is the man who trusts me, GOD, the woman who sticks with GOD ... Serene and calm through droughts, bearing fresh fruit every season" (Jeremiah 17:7–8 MSG).

So, how do I stick with Jesus? I proclaim I'm sticking with Jesus: *Jesus, I'm sticking with You. I'm giving You what I don't understand and can't fix. I'm giving You what I don't like about me, my husband, and my marriage. I'm positioning myself to hear Your truth, to talk to others who love You, and to read wise instruction from good books—most importantly, the Bible. And even if it kills me, I'm not throwing orange juice today. Amen.*

Yes, Jesus loves those in messy marriages.

Lord, today I'm going to hold my temper, hold my tongue, and hold Your truth. In Jesus' name, Amen.

REMEMBER

Honest cries for help lifted up to Jesus will not go unheard.

REFLECT

Where do you generally go after a heated argument with your husband? Do you run to your mother or a friend to discuss it, or do you turn to Jesus and the Bible for truth?

RESPOND

Right now, remember all the reasons you admire, appreciate, and love your husband. Think of the big and small ones, like how he keeps his nails cut clean. File these away in your heart so the next time you are furious with him, you remember these reasons you love him, and you allow love to overtake your anger.

POWER VERSES

Psalm 62:8; Psalm 146:5

Knowing God by Name*

God's names are a promise of who He is. Thank You Lord, that You are:

- *Emmanuel*: My God with Me (Matthew 1:22–23)
- *El-Channun*: The Gracious God (Jonah 4:2)
- *El Hanne'eman*: The Faithful God (Deuteronomy 7:9)
- *El Roi*: The God Who Sees Me (Genesis 16:13–14)
- *El ha-Gibbor*: The Mighty God, God the Hero (Isaiah 9:6)
- *El Shaddai*: The All-Sufficient God (Genesis 17:1–2)
- *El Sali*: God of My Strength (Psalm 42:9)
- *El Olam*: The Everlasting God (Genesis 21:32–33)
- *El Elyon*: The Most High God (Daniel 4:34)
- *Elohim*: God, My Mighty Creator (Genesis 1:1)
- *Jehovah Jireh*: The Lord Who Will Provide for Me (Genesis 22:13–14)
- *Jehovah Rapha*: The Lord Who Heals Me (Exodus 15:26)
- *Jehovah Nissi*: The Lord My Banner (Exodus 17:15–16)
- *Jehovah Shalom*: The Lord My Peace (Judges 6:24)
- *Yahweh Tsuri*: The Lord My Rock (Psalm 144:1)
- *Jehovah Rohi*: The Lord My Shepherd (Psalm 23:1)
- *Jehovah Shammah*: The Lord Is There for Me (Ezekiel 48:35)
- *Abba*: My Father (Psalm 68:5–6)

---

*This is taken from Renee Swope's book *A Confident Heart* (Revell, 2011). Renee's passion is to help women live confidently in Christ by showing them how to *rely on* and *live in* the security of God's promises in their everyday lives.

Bible Versions

Scripture quotations marked AMP are taken from *The Amplified Bible*. Copyright © 1954, 1958, 1962, 1964, 1965, 1987 by The Lockman Foundation. All rights reserved. Used by permission.

Scripture quotations marked ESV are taken from *The Holy Bible, English Standard Version,* copyright © 2001 by Crossway Bibles, a division of Good News Publishers. Used by permission. All rights reserved.

Scripture quotations marked GW are taken from the *God's Word® Translation*. Copyright © 1995 by God's Word to the Nations. Published by Green Key Books. Used by permission.

Scripture quotations marked KJV are taken from the King James Version of the Bible.

Scripture quotations marked MSG are taken from *The Message*. Copyright © 1993, 1994, 1995, 1996, 2000, 2001, 2002. Used by permission of NavPress Publishing Group.

Scripture quotations marked NASB are taken from the *New American Standard Bible*. Copyright © 1960, 1962, 1963, 1968, 1971, 1972, 1973, 1975, 1977, 1995 by The Lockman Foundation. Used by permission.

Scripture quotations marked NIrV are taken from the Holy Bible*, New International Reader's Version®, NIrV®*. Copyright © 1995, 1996, 1998 by Biblica, Inc™. Used by permission of Zondervan. All rights reserved worldwide.

Scripture quotations marked NLT are taken from the *Holy Bible, New Living Translation,* copyright © 1996, 2004. Used by permission of Tyndale House Publishers, Inc., Wheaton, Illinois. All rights reserved.

Meet the Authors

Renee Swope is Proverbs 31 Ministries' executive director of radio and development, and served as senior editor of *Encouragement for Today* devotions for the past several years. She's also the best-selling and award-winning author of *A Confident Heart*, cohost of Proverbs 31 Ministries' radio show, and a national conference speaker. Renee's passion is to help women live confidently in Christ by showing them how to rely on and live in the security of God's promises in their everyday lives. She loves to help women discover that they already have what it takes to become all that God created them to be. She'd love to connect with and encourage you on her blog at *www.reneeswope.com*.

Lysa TerKeurst is a *New York Times* best-selling author, national speaker, and president of Proverbs 31 Ministries. You can read her daily blog at *www.LysaTerKeurst.com* or hear her encouragement through the Proverbs 31 radio program played on over 1,200 outlets. Lysa loves that the first four letters of *Messiah* spell "mess" because all of her messages come from her awareness of what a mess she can be. Most days you can find her writing from her sticky farm table in North Carolina where she lives with her husband, Art, her five priority blessings—Jackson, Mark, Hope, Ashley, and Brooke, three dogs, and a mouse that refuses to leave her kitchen.

Samantha Evilsizer especially enjoys studying the Word and putting it into practice with her amazing husband, Joshua. She carries a running list of words whose meanings she plans to look up, particularly words in the original Greek and Hebrew Scriptures. She serves as coeditor of *Encouragement for Today* devotions and social media coordinator for Proverbs 31 Ministries, and writes on her blog at *www.samanthaevilsizer.org*.

Meet the Contributing Writers

Wendy Blight is a wife, mother, author, speaker, and Bible teacher. Her passion is to help women gain confidence that they can tackle any problem life presents through God's Word. Through Bible study, she equips a woman how to (1) identify Scriptures that address pressing issues in her life, (2) understand how those Scriptures apply, and (3) personalize and pray those Scriptures to bring restoration and transformation. Learn more at *http://wendyblight.com*.

Micca Campbell is a national women's conference speaker with Proverbs 31 Ministries and the author of *An Untroubled Heart*. Micca is passionate about reaching the unsaved with the life-changing message of Jesus Christ and helping women fear less and live more abundantly in Christ. From her cowboy boots to her Southern roots, she's proud to be a country girl. Micca and her family reside in Nashville, Tennessee. Visit Micca at *www.miccacampbell.com* and on Facebook and Twitter.

Amy Carroll's joy and passion is helping women find a deep connection to God's Word and to each other. She's committed to opening up her whole life, as her mentors have, to teach the lessons she's learned in her pursuit of applying God's truth. Amy is an ordinary woman who laughs at corny jokes, cries at Hallmark commercials, and is afraid of bouncing checks and of her own double chin. But she has a God-given ability to share His big truths in small, understandable bites. She loves Scripture and is dedicated to teaching it in all its unvarnished glory. To share life with Amy, join her at her blog at *www.amycarroll.org*.

Lynn Cowell's heartbeat is encouraging women to become wise and raise wiser daughters. Through her books, *His Revolutionary Love* and *Devotions for a Revolutionary Year* and her "Revolutionary Love" conferences, she empowers young women to find Jesus to be the filler of their love gap and the source of positive self-worth and confidence. Lynn lives in North Carolina with her husband, Greg, and their three children.

Her favorite day would include the mountains, a well-worn sweatshirt, and anything that combines chocolate and peanut butter. You can connect with Lynn at *www.lynncowell.com*.

Karen Ehman is the director of speakers for Proverbs 31 Ministries and a six-time author whose passion is to help women live their priorities and love their lives. Her latest book, entitled *LET. IT. GO.: How to Stop Running the Show and Start Walking in Faith*, is on the topic of how not to be a control freak. She has been the guest on national media outlets such as Focus on the Family, Moody Mid-day Connection, and The 700 Club. Married to her college sweetheart, Todd, for over twenty-five years, she is the mother of three sometimes ornery but mostly charming children. The Ehmans make their home in rural Michigan. Connect with her through her encouraging and practical blog at *www.karenehman.com*.

T. Suzanne Eller (Suzie) comes alongside women to gently lead them in a new direction. Sharing her own story, Suzie unpacks the transformation and healing that take place when you encounter a loving Savior. Suzie is an author of several books, an international speaker and Bible study teacher, mother, wife, and "Gramma." She has been the guest on media outlets such as Focus on the Family, Mid-day Connection, Aspiring Women, and The Harvest Show. Suzie would love you to drop in at her blog at *www.tsuzanneeller.com*.

Sharon Glasgow and her husband Dale live on a farm in Virginia, milking goats, gathering eggs, gardening, and homesteading. They have five grown daughters. Sharon is a vibrant international speaker, compelling audiences to understand their inheritance in Christ and how that empowers them. She has been on Proverbs 31 Ministries speaking team for over ten years. You can visit Sharon and her farm, see her favorite speaking topics, or hear what God is speaking to her on her blog at *www.sharonglasgow.com*.

Nicki Koziarz is a wife to Kris and mom to three fun girls, Taylor, Hope-Ann, and Kennedy. She is passionate about reaching those far from God because, by His scandalous grace, He brought her back to Him. Nicki is also an aspiring photographer and enjoys the perspective of life from behind the lens. You can stay connected with her by visiting her site at *www.nickikoziarz.com*.

Tracie Miles is a national conference speaker with Proverbs 31 Ministries and the author of *Stressed-Less Living: Finding God's Peace in Your Chaotic World*. Through her genuine transparency, humor, and Southern sincerity, Tracie speaks God's truths to empower and motivate women to depend on Christ in their everyday lives and to discover God's unshakable joy in the unpredictable journey of life. Her driving passion is to lead women to a deeper understanding of God's unconditional love and help them find peace and purpose through learning to live intentionally for Christ. Visit Tracie at *www.traciemiles.com*.

Rachel Olsen says, "The Bible holds the most sublime secrets—divine revelations every woman needs to know. It is simultaneously a love letter, a mirror, an instruction manual, and a window into our soul and God's heart." Rachel is an author and speaker with a passion for fostering focused life-change in Christ. She's the coauthor of *My One Word: Change Your Life with Just One Word*. Rachel blogs at *www.rachelolsen.com*.

Wendy Pope is a wife to Scott, mother to Blaire and Griffin, author, speaker, and Bible study teacher. Whether in the pulpit or on paper, her passion is biblical application. Wendy leads women all over the world to life-change through her in-depth online Bible studies. Witty and down to earth, she teaches with such transparency that every woman feels that Wendy is speaking directly to her heart. To learn more about Wendy or to join her online ministry, visit *www.wendypope.org*.

Luann Prater loves quality time with family and husband, Dwight. Her favorite title is Grandma. She is a Proverbs 31 speaker, writer, and national radio host of Encouragement Cafe with Luann & Friends. Luann squeezes joy out of each day, and then points others to the source of that joy: Jesus. Luann portrays hope from her own stained past and encourages women to shine God's brilliant glow of grace to a hurting world. Join her at *www.luannprater.com*.

Melissa Taylor is a leader, speaker, and encourager to whom women relate because she's not afraid to talk about real issues honestly. She leads online Bible studies on her blog because she wants to provide a venue of study for women who aren't in a Bible study group. Women are hungry for the Word of God and it is Melissa's goal to teach them how to live and apply it. Connect with Melissa and her Online Bible Studies at *www.melissataylor.org*.

Van Walton's childhood experiences in the Colombian jungles and Andes Mountains of South America laid the foundation for her passion to bring Jesus into the hearts of Latina women. Working with a team of translators and partnering with Proverbs 31 Ministries has turned her vision into a reality. Van, the author of *From the Pound to the Palace*, teaches in a Christian school, and writes and facilitates Bible studies in her community and church in Charlotte, North Carolina. Visit with Van at *www.vanwalton.com*.

Glynnis Whitwer is on staff with Proverbs 31 Ministries as the senior editor of the *P31 Woman* magazine and director of the writer's track for She Speaks. She is the author of three books, including *I Used to Be So Organized*, and coauthor of a Bible studies series entitled *Kingdom Living*. Her passion is to help women combine peace and productivity, thereby increasing their ability to live a sold-out life for Jesus Christ. She blogs regularly at *www.glynniswhitwer.com*, and loves to offer practical tips with a spiritual touch. Glynnis, her husband, Tod, and their five children (all teenagers and young adults) live in Glendale, Arizona.

About Proverbs 31 Ministries

If you were inspired by *Encouragement for Today* and desire to deepen your own personal relationship with Jesus Christ, we encourage you to connect with Proverbs 31 Ministries. Proverbs 31 Ministries exists to be a trusted friend who will take you by the hand and walk by your side, leading you one step closer to the heart of God through:

- *Encouragement for Today*, free online daily devotions
- Daily radio program
- Books and resources
- Dynamic speakers with life-changing messages
- Online communities
- Online Bible studies

To learn more about Proverbs 31 Ministries or to inquire about having one of our team members speak at your next event:

Call 1-877-P31-HOME
or visit *www.proverbs31.org*

Proverbs 31 Ministries
630 Team Road, Suite 100
Matthews, NC 28105
www.proverbs31.org

NIV Real-Life Devotional Bible for Women

This hardcover Bible will help you live up to your God-given potential. Insightful daily devotions written by the women at Proverbs 31 Ministries help you maintain life's balance in spite of today's hectic pace. Dive into the beauty and clarity of the NIV Bible text paired with daily devotions crafted by women just like you — women who want to live authentically and fully grounded in the Word of God.

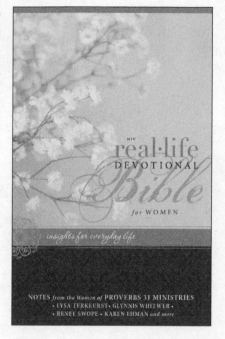

Available in stores and online!

Share Your Thoughts

With the Author: Your comments will be forwarded to the author when you send them to *zauthor@zondervan.com*.

With Zondervan: Submit your review of this book by writing to *zreview@zondervan.com*.

Free Online Resources at
www.zondervan.com

Daily Bible Verses and Devotions: Enrich your life with daily Bible verses or devotions that help you start every morning focused on God. Visit www.zondervan.com/newsletters.

Free Email Publications: Sign up for newsletters on Christian living, academic resources, church ministry, fiction, children's resources, and more. Visit www.zondervan.com/newsletters.

Zondervan Bible Search: Find and compare Bible passages in a variety of translations at www.zondervanbiblesearch.com.

Other Benefits: Register to receive online benefits like coupons and special offers, or to participate in research.